# The Beale Treasure Codes

# The Key

**Claudine Fulton Ellis**

Published by Goose Creek Valley Enterprises Vinton, Virginia 24179



ISBN 978-1-917007-32-0



Cover Design by Impress 'Em Products, Troutville, VA.

Interior Design Book Production and Copy Review by Golden Quill Press, Roanoke, VA

Editing by Bobbi R. Madry, Fort Wayne, IN

Published in Cooperation with Golden Quill Press Roanoke, Virginia 24011

# Table of Contents

# ACKNOWLEDGEMENTS

I cannot begin to thank all the individuals to whom I am indebted, but, certain obligations cannot be ignored. I wish to thank all the following for their contributions in helping me bring about the conclusion of this story. I am grateful to many people including: the late Mr. Seldon D. Nelms, (Uncle Nell), for having shared with me the stories about his grandfather Ebenezer (Eben) Nelms and Captain Beall; the late Mrs. Hale for helping me contact Eula Journell Patterson and her son Elwood Journell and to them both, for their involvement and contributions concerning the copy I made of the letter (key) to the treasure codes written by Thomas Jefferson Beall. And to others for their help: Mr. James Howell, and his wife the late Mrs. Howell, Burford's Tavern,(Locust Level), Montvale, V.A. for allowing Barbara Smith and me to tour the old tavern and sharing the story about the Beall ghost. Kitty Buford Pendleton kindly shared stories and photos at Buford's Tavern.

The late William E. Brugh, my brother-in-law, was very helpful in the research of the Brugh family genealogy and my son-in-law, the late William R. Ball III helped me on numerous occasions regarding my research. As were the late Horace Hood III and Stella Hood, members of the local Chapter of Archaeology regarding the grave site of George Rader Brugh. And thank you, to Mr. Albert Atwell, for his contribution made in the genealogy research of Thomas Jefferson Beall.

Supportive family and friends are so important in this type of project and mine have gone above and beyond. The late George Henegar was so helpful in showing me trails. He and his sister the late, Mildred Henegar Huffman were such special friends, who always encouraged me to keep looking and to one day write this story. The late Jerry Hayes, also a dear life-long friend has given me support and encouragement, as has Raymond S. Clark.

To all the members of my family, a very special thank you for your enduring support and encouragement. My nieces, Brenda F. Booker and Jeana Azar as well as my daughters, Deborah Ellis Painter and Julia Ellis Ball, all gave me invaluable support. My thanks also to Angela Dooley, my granddaughter, who was my personal secretary and typed and retyped on demand.

This acknowledgement wouldn't be complete without a very special thank you to my dear and loving husband, the late James Ellis for all the years he was there for me. And I thank God, most of all, for having given me the time I needed and a mind with which to write this story. Amen.

# INTRODUCTION

You, the reader, are about to embark on a true and fascinating account of my lifetime involvement with the Beall Treasure Codes. To better understand my journey, I have included, "The Beale Papers." These documents will introduce Thomas Jefferson Beall and his associates who were said to have found great treasure: gold, silver and precious jewels. This treasure was also supposedly hidden in the Blue Ridge Mountains of Virginia, somewhere near Buford's Tavern, in Bedford County. And that is where I come in...

When you begin to read my story you will see how, at every turn of my life, this story has followed me; even pursued me. From my first psychic experience to decades later, everything I've experienced and learned has led me to tell this story.

You will notice two different spellings: Beall and Beale. For the purposes of my story Beall, will be used, as that is the original spelling I encountered.

With the help of my family, friends and people I contacted over the years, I now feel that I can tell my story.

# PROLOGUE

In 1822 Thomas Jefferson Beall stayed at the Washington Hotel in Lynchburg, Virginia on his way out west. Before he set out on his expedition, he gave the hotel proprietor, Mr. Morriss, a locked iron box—as well as very specific instructions regarding the box and its contents. "If I do not return by the time ten years pass to reclaim the box, you are to break the lock and open the box. Inside you will find important papers of value."

Mr. Morriss put the box away and didn't do anything further about it. Twenty-three years later he remembered the box. He assumed by then that Beall was never coming back — probably dead—so he opened the box.

Inside he found three papers filled with numbers and a letter written in English. The letter detailed the story of Beall's finding a remarkable treasure and the written "key" that would decipher the papers with numbers that would lead to the location of the treasure.

Morriss was taken aback. He had waited an additional ten years, but never received any "key." Mr. Morriss attempted to decode the ciphers without the "key," but was unsuccessful. He was in failing health and finally decided to give the iron box and its contents to his friend, James B. Ward, also of Lynchburg, Virginia.

James Ward worked on the ciphers and was successful in deciphering the paper marked, "2" using the Declaration of Independence for the Thirteen colonies of the United States of America. He was unsuccessful regarding, ciphers "1" and "3."

In 1864, Ward compiled a historical account of the Beall Treasure, called, "The Beale Papers." In 1885, Ward had the Virginia Book and

Print Job Co, in Lynchburg print "The Beale Papers," in pamphlet form. Before the printing was completed, a fire mysteriously broke out and destroyed all but a few copies.

In 1964, The Roanoke City Library placed an ad in the Roanoke Times advertising the sale of, "The Beale Papers." The name "Beale," even though spelled differently from the Beall spelling I was familiar with, was enough for me to purchase a copy. After reading "The Beale Papers," I am certain that I found the "key!"

"The Beale Papers" at the end of this book are being reprinted in their original format. Any grammatical or spelling errors have not been altered to preserve the authenticity of these papers.

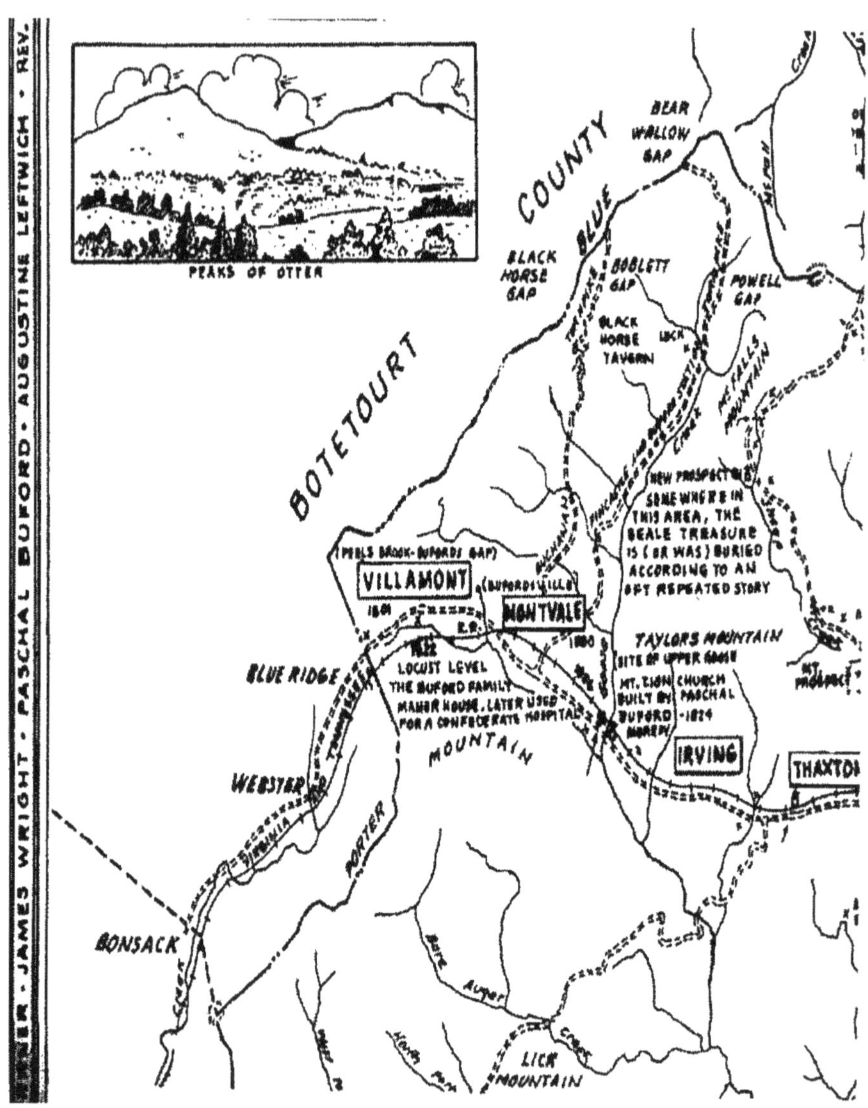


PEAKS OF OTTER

# CHAPTER ONE

## Buford's Airfield

Long before I came to Montvale, formerly Bufordville, in Goose Creek Valley, Bedford County, Virginia, its early inhabitants the Sioux Indians, the Bufords (Bueafords) from England, and Thomas Jefferson Beall, had all come and gone — but not without leaving behind traces and echoes of their lives lived there.

I closed my eyes, and journeyed back through the years to the summer of 1938 in Goose Creek Valley, Virginia. I was five years old and my family would go to Buford's Airfield, to watch the aerial shows. At that time the field was only a small dirt landing strip, surrounded by the Buford farmlands. Mr. Buford participated in the aerial shows and my father Benjamin Fulton, was a friend of his. Mr. Buford took great pride in his ability to perform fancy stunts for the crowds of people that watched from the roadside on Route 460 East. My father liked to fly with James Buford, and my mother and I would watch with great anticipation as they performed their stunts. I felt it would be great fun to fly in the plane with them, so every Sunday, Id plead with my mother, but she always replied, "No, you are too young." I suppose, on this particular Sunday afternoon she finally got tired of my pleading, and finally gave in. The big moment of my life had finally come: I was going to fly at last!

My father was holding my hand as we crossed the airfield to where Mr. Buford was waiting in his airplane. As we got close the noise from the plane's engine was so loud it hurt my ears. We boarded the plane, and my father sat me in a small seat directly behind Mr. Buford; buckled me in tightly, then seated himself up front beside his friend. I thought with great expectations, "Now, at last, I am going to fly!"

The plane started moving-- slowly at first and then faster and faster until we raced across the airfield. Suddenly, I felt the plane lift up from the ground. Up, up into the air we rose. It was a wonderful feeling indeed! Next we leveled off and Mr. Buford shouted over the noise to ask my father if he was ready for a few figure eight's. My father turned back to look at me and nodded.

Suddenly the plane was down, then up and upside down and sideways, all to perform this figure eight stunt, But after several of these, my father noticed that I was getting air sick and had Buford take me down.

After we landed, Mr. Buford and my father helped me off the plane and I found myself facing the direction of the old Buford Tavern and Locust Level, an old brick dwelling located at the edge of the airfield. I knew absolutely nothing about those two structures or what would follow that day.

# CHAPTER TWO

## My First Psychic Experience

That day at Buford's airfield as I stood facing Buford's Tavern, suddenly I saw a young woman. She was standing on the lower level of the back porch of the old brick dwelling known as Locust Level which stood at the edge of the airfield. There weren't any signs but I knew those were the names of the buildings. The porch appeared to be constructed of wood that had been painted white, and had white columns and railings with an architectural scroll design.

The young woman was tall and slender. Her black hair was pulled back from her face and appeared to be gathered up at the back of her head. I could see that her eyes were brown. She was a standing there with both arms outstretched toward me.

The woman wore a full-skirted gray dress with long sleeves and a long white apron. The cuffs on the sleeves and collar of her dress were also white, like a Pilgrim style of dress. As I was observing her, I began to experience a powerful flow of love between us that seemed to bond us together. I felt a very strong connection, as if she was my mother. The desire to be with her was overwhelming. I started to run to her, but my father caught up with me and reached for me. I stumbled and fell face forward to the ground. When I fell I looked up and saw myself standing there, dressed in a long white dress made out of white eyelet material, with a square neckline in front, full puffed sleeves just above the elbows, and a blue satin ribbon encircling the waistline. Also a bow tied in the front with ribbons streaming down either side almost touching the hemline of the dress. I couldn't understand what was happening, but then my father lifted me from the ground to a standing position. I was crying and screaming, "I want my mother! She's standing on the porch," all the while pointing to the old house of Locust Level. My father tried to comfort me and reassure me that my mother was waiting in the car for us, but I didn't want to be comforted.

I kicked and screamed, "I want my mother! She's standing on the porch!" But my father just picked me up and carried me back to where the car was parked on Route 460 East. When we reached the car, my father put me in the back seat and got in and started up the motor. My mother turned around to look at me and tried to calm me down. She couldn't understand why I was so upset and why I was saying these things about another mother. As my father drove us out of sight, I felt as if that was my mother I was leaving behind, which didn't make any sense as I was looking at my mother in the front seat. I turned to watch the lady standing on the back porch of Locust Level. As she disappeared from sight, somehow I knew I had two mothers, and I didn't want to leave the one on the back porch behind. I vowed, "Someday, when I grow up, I will come back here."

My father continued to fly from time to time with James Buford, but he never took me to Buford's Airfield again.

# CHAPTER THREE

## My Second Psychic Experience

In the summer of 1939, my family visited my aunt and uncle, Oscar and Booksie Arthur. They lived on a large farm in Bedford County, Virginia, that still showed signs of ruts from a once well-traveled trail. My aunt referred to this as, "The Old Great Trail Road."

Their children were closer in age to my sister Lillian, who was 18, and my brothers Benjie, 13 and Orina 24. It was extremely hot and we all wanted to go for a swim. We went down to my cousins' favorite swimming hole at Little Otter River. Being older they were able to swim in the deeper waters, but I was so young, I had to remain where the water was shallow. I explored this area of the water and discovered it was where the Old Great Trail Road my aunt had mentioned crossed the Little Otter River.

I didn't have a bathing suit so after wading in and watching the others swim, I became bored and lonely and decided to return to my aunt's farmhouse about one-half mile up a hill. I turned to go, but the shallow water appeared to be getting deeper and it was freezing! I grabbed my dress at the hemline and gathered it up above my knees to keep it from getting wet. The water started to swirl around and around like a whirlpool! I stood transfixed; gazing into the water. I saw the legs of horses begin to materialize. I continued staring, as the horses became totally visible. I could see four in all. All were black and pulling as hard as they could to free a covered wagon from the mire. Then I saw another covered wagon with its team of four black horses materialize on the bank, waiting its turn to cross the river. The first wagon directly in front of me appeared to be so heavily weighed down, and it was stuck in the mud. The horses were trying hard, but could not free the heavy load. Then two men appeared; they were dressed in black, wearing large-brimmed hats and tight-fitted boots that came up to their knees. I watched as they stood in front of the horses, pulling and struggling hard on the reins to help move them forward. Having no success, they moved to the back of the wagon where they pushed with all their might. All their efforts to move the team and wagon were futile. I watched as the two men unloaded the stuck wagon. They carried bars of gold that seemed very heavy to the opposite side of the river. When the men had finished carrying the gold to the other side of the river, the team of horses was able to pull the wagon out of the mud. Now with their wagon and its precious cargo safely on the other side, the men reloaded their gold into the wagon. The men then turned their attention back to the second wagon that had been waiting to cross the river.

During all this time, I'd become so spellbound by this vision, that I was unable to move from the spot where I stood in the water. I continued to watch as the men crossed the river back and forth; their arms loaded down with gold from the second wagon, until the second wagon was emptied sufficiently to maneuver it across the river without becoming stuck. Then the men took the horses' reins and slowly pulled the wagon across the river to the other side. This time I was fascinated as I watched the men reload their gold cargo. I didn't know about gold, but I sensed that it was very valuable.

I knew it had only been a short time that I was standing in the water, but it must have taken hours for these two men to unload and reload the two wagons and then cross the river. Something made me continue to stand there. The men appeared to be weary and moved more slowly along the trail as they climbed the hill just in front of me. The trail turned and crossed a section of what I recognized as the yard at my aunt and uncle's farmhouse. I watched as the wagons left the yard and rumbled and swayed slowly moving ove rough terrain, as the wagons continued on the old trail until they were out of my sight.

I stood mesmerized for a moment then turned and ran back to the farmhouse. When I got to the yard I stopped. My mind filled with questions, *What was happening to me and who were these men and...?* So many thoughts I didn't understand. I looked around and decided not to tell anyone, but I made a vow that when I grew up I would come back and try to find these men and follow their wagons of gold to wherever they went.

# CHAPTER FOUR

## Visions At The Harshbarger-Munger House

In the fall of 1939, vows I had made after my vision at the Little Otter River began to come to fruition at a house located on the Harshbarger Road in the County of Roanoke, Virginia.

One Sunday afternoon in mid-September, I went with my parents to look at the old vacant house known as the Harshbarger-Munger House. The tall dead grass and weeds gave the appearance that no one had lived there for quite some time. The house was a large two-story structure built out of huge chestnut logs that had been painted a drab gray. Colonial brick chimneys stood tall at either end of the house and a wide front porch was centered in the middle. When we walked up on the front porch, my eyes were drawn to the large colonial door. As I stood there peeking through the glass pane centered in the middle of the door, my eyes were drawn to a staircase. Suddenly, I became aware of a spiritual presence; a man who I felt had died in this house long ago. I knew that he was somehow connected with the vision I had experienced at Little Otter River and the men transferring the bars of gold back and forth to free their wagons. Just as suddenly as he appeared—he was gone! The sensation had also passed and all I could think of was, *What does all of this mean?*

I looked around. My parents were busy looking at the Harshbarger-Munger house property and didn't notice anything strange about me. I decided to go exploring, but something was drawing me toward a large weather-beaten barn on the property. The barn was built partly over the high cliff of rocks that overlooked Carvin's Creek. Along the creek and across the property were the remains of an old trail road. The old weathered barn stood on an incline and extended out over the old trail with the open end being supported by posts. The floor of the barn on that side served as the roof of an open shelter.

I felt compelled to go inside. The barn was divided into five large sections. One section was a small room with a wooden bench attached to the side of one wall. I became aware of this room being used as a waiting room for stagecoach travelers. Then I heard my mother calling.

Later that month, we moved into the Harshbarger-Munger House.

# CHAPTER FIVE

## Vision Of Mr. Brugh's Death

One weekend winter's day in 1944, when I was eleven, I was seated at a little table and had been looking out of the second-floor window of our home. I wished it weren't so cold so my mother would let me go out to play. When I turned away from the window, I saw the apparitions of two men. When I looked around the room the furnishings had changed from ours to something from an earlier time period. It dawned on me that five years earlier, when we came to look at the then Harshbarger-Munger house, this was the same room on the second floor where I had first felt a presence of the spirit of a man I believed died in the house.

One of the men had an olive complexion, wavy black hair, and brown eyes. He was tall, thin, and quite handsome. He wore a white shirt with full, long sleeves much like that of a pirate's shirt and his trousers were a dark blue, almost black. He was standing beside a high-posted brass bed, looking down at the other man who appeared very still, as though sleeping. The man turned from the bed and crossed the room to the window opposite of where I was sitting. I watched in amazement as he went over to the window—raised it and then climbed out. I couldn't understand why he'd leave the room that way when he could have used the staircase.

I got up from my chair and went over to the window. It should have been cold, but it wasn't. And the trees I saw had blossoms and they were not the same as trees in our yard that year of 1944. I looked out the window trying to see where the man might have gone. Suddenly, I sensed that Indians had killed him not far from this house.

I turned back to the brass bed where the other man appeared to be asleep. Looking down at him, I wondered who he was and why he hadn't moved. Then, as if answering my question, it was mentally revealed to me that this man had been murdered—suffocated with a bed pillow. The man who had just left the room had befriended him, yet for some reason unknown to me, he had also taken his life.

*Oh, God! I thought. How horrible that anyone could do such an awful thing!*

I fixed my eyes on the man I now knew for sure was murdered. He was of stocky build with dark graying hair and a full beard. The man was wearing a long sleeve multi-colored plaid shirt. While I stood watching him, a wooden high-back chair became visible beside the bed. On the chair was a pair of dark-colored trousers with pockets that were turned inside-out and empty. More questions flooded my mind. *Who is he? And why was he murdered?* At that moment, the name Brugh was revealed to me and the fact that he'd never married but had lived in a place like this old house—a place where travelers would stop and stay the night. His father had been a merchant who sold pots and pans from his wagons on the old trails and gave his son horses and wagons to go west. I also began to understand that Mr. Brugh's family had never known about his ill-fated death.

I felt compelled to go back to the window. When I looked across the field behind the house, I saw an area that I perceived to be Mr. Brugh's unmarked grave. I sensed that he'd been buried as one might bury a dog. As I stood there experiencing overwhelming compassion for him, the doorway of the room was suddenly filled with a spiritual presence! I did not see anything with my eyes, but I could see the spirit in my mind. I felt a large, formless cloud that was all white. As the spirit glided over to my table I could feel a gentleness and I wasn't afraid. I knew immediately this was the same spirit I had encountered in 1939 when I first visited to the old Harshbarger-Munger house. The spirit moved slowly into the room and stood next to me. "Go into the attic," it instructed me. "You will find something very valuable."

# CHAPTER SIX

## Spirit Leads To The Bible

The Harshbarger-Munger house always held strange happenings for me, but today, sitting on the second floor of the house that we now lived in, I was mesmerized as the spirit's vision faded into the air. It took me a few minutes to comprehend the message I'd just received from the spirit, "Go into the attic," it instructed me, "You will find something very valuable."

I knew I was going to follow its directions and go into the attic. Even though I wasn't frightened, I still said a prayer, "I will go in the name of Jesus."

On my way to the attic, I had to walk past a dresser with a mirror. I was stunned to see my reflection in the mirror wearing a beautiful gold necklace with alternate rows of rubies and diamonds! The necklace was fashioned in the design of a bib. I clutched my neck with both hands and looked down, but there was no such necklace. I looked back to the mirror, but this time only my image was reflected. I wondered, Could that be what I was going to discover in the attic? I realized that was silly. Who would leave such a beautiful piece of jewelry in a dirty old attic?

When I got to the attic stairs, I reached up to open the attic door. I had to push hard to open it. When I pushed myself up onto the attic floor, my hand sank into a kind of black dust that completely covered my hand. At that instant, my hand made an electrifying contact with something on the floor. A shocking sensation ran through my hand and up my arm. I knew that whatever lay beneath my hand was what the spirit had led me to find. Slowly, I brushed the black dust from side to side until I could see what appeared to be a large book without a front cover. I picked the book up and sat on the attic step to examine it.

The book was an old Bible. When I placed the bible upright between my knees, it fell open revealing two sheets of paper. One sheet of paper had a hand-drawn map; the other sheet was a neatly handwritten letter. Across the top of the letter was written, "The Declaration of Independence." It was dated May 15th, and was signed by Thomas Jefferson Beall. The paper was from another time, as was the way the words were written. As best I can tell, it said:

*"May 15, 1852*

*The Declaration of Independence*

*We, the undersigned delegates in general assembly, assembled in the House of Burgesses this day, have been advised by the good people of the United States of America, to publish and declare that these united colonies are and of right ought to be free and independent states, and for the rectitude of our intentions, let facts be deemed to a candid world. "Traitor, Traitor! Let the traitor be hung! 'HE has burnt our towns and murdered the lives of our people. He has made judges dependent on his will alone and for the tenure and pay for their office. "Caesar had His Brutus and King George the third, his Cromwell."*

In addition to the letter, there was an empty white envelope with the following message printed in manuscript on the front: *"Not to be delivered until June 1832."*

I could read the words: Taxes, Boston Tea Party, Religious freedom, Cutting off trade with other parts of the world, and All men are created equal by the creator, and then the last paragraph read:

*"With a firm resolve for the protection of divine providence, we mutually pledge to each other our lives, our fortunes, and our sacred*

*honor."*

The signature was written neatly underneath the last line of his letter, as if he had not wanted it to be easily seen.

*"Thomas Jefferson Beall"*

Written at the bottom of his letter were three columns of men's names. Some of the names I recognized were: James Madison, James Mason, George Wythe, Edmond Pendleton, Richard Henry Lee, and Patrick Henry.

I looked through the Bible and found a list of twenty-five or thirty names and addresses written on some of the blank pages near the back of the Bible. The first name was Ms. Mary, Richmond, Virginia. The second name was Ms. Mary Elizabeth, Lynchburg, Virginia. There were other names: Obenchain, Buford, Hart, Nininger, and Otey. I read Mr. Beall's letter several times, but I was unable to understand its meaning.

I decided to show the Bible with its contents to my mother. I left the attic and ran into the kitchen to announce my find. My mother was kneading dough, and too busy to pay attention to me. When she finally understood what I'd been up to, she scolded me for snooping around where I had "no business" and ordered me to put everything back. I begged her to allow me to keep the mysterious Bible; even just for a little while. She finally listened as I explained what I'd read. Mother found it puzzling too and finally agreed to let me keep the Bible for a few days anyway, but only if I were very careful not to disturb the contents.

I kept Beall's Bible in my dresser drawer. One day my sister, Esterlene, and I had a heated argument and she ran into my bedroom, grabbed the Bible from my dresser, and started to tear the letter. I ran to stop her, but she had already torn the right side of the letter halfway down. I had no tape to repair Beall's letter, so I just returned it to the Bible.

I knew I had to keep Mr. Beall's letter safe, so the following week, I worked diligently until I finished copying the letter. I also tried to copy his map, with no success. I placed my copy of the letter (three sheets of paper with one sheet of clean paper folded around them) in a white envelope and wrote in large letters the word "IMPORTANT," across the front. I did not sign my copy of Beall's letter with my name or his. I knew I had to find a safe hiding place, so I hid my copy behind the fireplace mantle in the room where I'm sure Mr. Brugh had been murdered. Since this was also where the spiritual presence had appeared to lead me to the Bible in the attic, it seemed a perfect place.

One day, for a reason I do not know, my mother insisted it was time I put the Bible back. She watched from the bottom of the attic stairs as I returned Beall's Bible with its original contents to where I had found them.

# CHAPTER SEVEN:
## Spirit Beckons Me To Mr. Brugh's Grave

One hot summer's day, shortly after my mother had me return the Beall Bible to the attic, I had another encounter with the same spiritual presence. I'd decided to go fishing. After digging for worms, I took my fishing pole and headed to my favorite fishing spot. The fish just weren't biting, and I finally decided to return home. On my way back, I decided to walk over by way of the old trail road. I approached the crest of the hill, and the spirit appeared in front of me!

I sensed it wanted me to follow. The spirit led me to the same place I'd seen from the bedroom window where I believed Mr. Brugh had been murdered. I stood there staring at the ground; I felt like this was the place where Mr. Brugh must have been buried, and not with any human dignity. I searched on the ground for some sort of marker, but there was none. I felt badly for him and decided, *Someday I would come back and dig him up and find his family so he could be buried with them.*

I looked around and found some fence posts that were in line with where I thought his grave might be. Then suddenly my thoughts were disrupted by another vision. Mr. Brugh was seated in a stagecoach being drawn by a team of black horses racing across a field of wild daisies. I could feel myself sitting in the stagecoach with Mr. Brugh, and I detected the sweet fragrance of the daisies. It flashed across my mind that Mr. Brugh was racing to his death at this old house.

Just then, someone shouted my name and jolted me from the vision. It was our neighbor, Mr. Nelms, "Deanie, come over here this minute!"

I gathered myself together and walked over to the fence that separated our properties and climbed over at the corner post. I crossed his back yard and walked to the back porch where he was standing. "What do you want, Mr. Nelms?" I asked.

"What are you doing out there in that field?" he questioned.

I was curious as to why he'd ask me such a question when the field is part of the property where I live. "Well, Mr. Nelms, you know I live over there," I replied.

"I don't want to see you out there messing around anymore," he lectured.

When I asked him why, he replied, "A man is buried out there somewhere in that field."

"Well, I didn't see any gravestone. Why are you so sure there's a grave in that field?" I asked.

Mr. Nelms looked straight at me and in a very stern voice said, "Never you mind! Just do as I say!" I realized Mr. Nelms knew about Mr. Brugh's death!

# CHAPTER EIGHT
## The Treasure Vault Is Revealed

I had heeded Mr. Nelms' warning about staying out of the field where I thought Mr. Brugh was buried. But on another summer's day in 1947, I was playing not far from our house near a part of the old trail road that ran alongside Carvin's Creek, when suddenly the spirit appeared again! Again, it wanted me to follow. This time it led me to a stone formation in a nearby cliff of rocks. The spirit made me understand there was a place similar to this one in a distant mountain, and pots of gold were buried there. A vision of that site flashed across my mind, and I was able to see a large, flat, gray stone recessed into the mountainside. There were two large openings on either side, and directly over the left entrance, there was another large stone, about three feet high. I understood this stone had been used as a marker to identify this formation from some distance away. I heard the spirit in my mind, "When you stand before that place, you will know it, for there is no other place like it in all of the mountains."

As the vision faded, I experienced a pulling sensation from behind and turned around to see a distant range of mountains that I knew as the Read Mountain area. Once again, I had the feeling that one day I would go in search of that place.

Soon after that experience, I was passing our basement door when I felt the presence of the spirit again. It indicated mentally there was something in the basement the spirit wanted me to see. The basement door was locked, so I crawled through a small window near the ground that was unlocked. Once I was inside the basement, there was just barely enough light to see. I followed the spirit to the wall opposite the window where three stones had fallen out and lay on the dirt floor. I felt cold air coming from the opening. *How could that be?* I left the basement and ran to tell my mother what I'd found.

"This must be why my bedroom above the basement area is always so cold!" I told her. My family didn't use the basement, and mother was upset with me that I'd gone down there. She handed me a small empty metal bucket and instructed me to go to the bank on the lower side of our yard and fill it with red clay dirt. She told me to mix the dirt with some water to make a mortar. After I had done that, she went with me to the basement. She turned on a flashlight so we could see the stone wall and the opening the fallen stones had made. We looked into the opening and could see beyond to what looked like an underground tunnel. While the cold air from the tunnel blew into my face, I replaced one stone at a time and smoothed out the red clay around each addition. In a short time, I'd repaired the stone wall with my homemade red clay mortar and the stones so that the wall was solid again.

# CHAPTER NINE
## The Rainbow Experience

It was a typical summer day in 1947. The day had been hot, and when a light shower began to fall, it made the air feel much cooler. I went out to stand on the back porch of our home. Looking at the Read Mountain range, I could see traces of an old trail road winding its way up the mountain. I watched the rainfall and thought of the spiritual presence that had told me about that place. I thought, *"Will I ever stand before that place and know what is revealed behind the stone?"*

The rain began to lessen, and as the sky cleared, I beheld the most vivid colors. I watched in amazement as the colors formed a rainbow right over the trail in the Read Mountain range. The rainbow formed its great arch, and I could see it moving in the direction of my house. I ran from the back porch to the front yard. The rainbow was now directly over my house; its form had finished right in our front yard!

The colors faded above me in mid-air. I ran around in circles, looking up all the while, until I could see directly up into the glorious array of the rainbow's colors. I stood transfixed as I gazed up into one of God's magnificent creations. I sensed a strange bonding with the rainbow. I looked toward the mountain range, but I knew I would have to go beyond Read Mountain to find the pots of gold. I thought, *"Maybe this rainbow is a sign, like in the Bible; a covenant."* I prayed, "Lord, will I ever stand before that place, as I was told I would?" As the rainbow and the sensations faded away, I had a strong feeling that someday I would.

# CHAPTER TEN

## Leaving The Harshbarger-Munger House

My family had gotten friendly with our neighbors, Mr. and Mrs. Nelms. When Mrs. Nelms died suddenly, Mr. Nelms was heartbroken. Mother would invite him to eat his evening meals on the weekends with my family. One night, Mr. Nelms told my father he planned to rent his home. He said he just couldn't bear to be alone in his house. My father was interested in renting the place, and that evening the two of them reached an agreement.

It was only a few weeks before the Christmas of 1947 when we moved into Mr. Nelms' home and became his surrogate family. Leaving the Harshbarger-Munger house was difficult for me. I wasn't allowed to go back into the attic and had to leave behind Mr. Beall's Bible with its letter and map. I also left my copy of his letter that I had hidden behind the fireplace mantle in the room where I believe Mr. Brugh had met his ill-fated death. I hoped that someday when I was older, I would discover what the letter meant, and at that time go back and recover it and I wondered whether I'd then discover the secrets that house held.

Mr. Nelms soon became one of our family; we all called him "Uncle Nell." One afternoon, Uncle Nell and I were sitting on the front porch sharing the newspaper. He started to talk about when my family had lived at the Harshbarger-Munger house. "Deanie, do you remember ever seeing a letter with the name of Thomas Jefferson Beall signed to it?"

"How do you spell the last name?" I asked, surprised by his question. I wanted to be sure before I answered.

"B-e-a-l-l," Uncle Nell replied. "It may have been just in a list of words — so think hard. It's very important!"

I was going to tell him how I'd found Mr. Beall's Bible, the letter with the signature and the hand-drawn map, but as I opened my mouth to speak, I had a strong sense that I shouldn't tell Uncle Nell, so I didn't.

He continued talking, all the while holding two fingers of his right hand tightly together in an upright position and gesturing to make his point. "My grandfather and Captain Beall were very close friends," he told me. "In fact, Beall had five brothers, but he was not as close them as he was to my grandfather."

"Uncle Nell," I asked, "was Captain Beall in the military?"

"As far as I know, he hadn't served, but he'd been the leader of a large party of men who'd chosen to call him "Captain Beall." Uncle Nell sat quietly for a moment as if reminiscing. "I remember my granddaddy, Eben Nelms, Captain Beall, and my grandfather had been with a large party of men in wild territory somewhere out West. The men on horseback had gone into a ravine, only to discover there was no way out. From high above them, a large group of Indians painted for war swooped down on them in a surprise attack. The Indians shot hundreds of arrows down on the trapped men. Men all around my grandfather were being wounded and killed. An arrow pierced his right hip, and he saw his end in sight when Captain Beall came to his rescue. He pulled his injured friend over to a large boulder and safety. From behind this stone, they both watched helplessly as their remaining wounded comrades lay helplessly pleading for mercy. But their cries were unheard by the band of savage Indians who scalped them. The Indians rounded up all the horses before leaving. Captain Beall took care of Grandpa's flesh wound, but without a horse, they didn't have much hope of getting out of the ravine alive.

On the third morning after the massacre, miraculously Captain Beall's faithful horse returned and found them behind the large stone. According to Uncle Nell, they were able to escape on horseback, but it took months for his grandfather and Captain Beall to return to Virginia.

"Some time later, Captain Beall visited Grandpa Eben with two other companions at the Harshbarger-Munger House. The men spent the night and then started out on what was to be Captain Beall's third trip out West." Uncle Nell stopped for a second. A sad look came over his face as he continued, "Grandfather stood in the doorway of the kitchen, which at that time was located in the basement of the old house, and waved goodbye to Beall and the others until they were out of sight. The men were traveling over the old Carvin's Trail Road, which ran alongside Carvin's Creek and went over to the James River.

"A month later, in May, Grandfather was traveling over the same section of Carvin's Trail Road that led to the James River, but before reaching the river, he spotted some abandoned wagons not far from the trail road. After making a close investigation, he was certain the wagons were Captain Beall's."

"Uncle Nell," I asked, "how could your grandfather have been sure those wagons belonged to Captain Beall?"

"You see, my grandfather had told me that Captain Beall hunted white buffalo. He brazenly displayed the hides all over his wagons. So when grandpa came across the wagons with the white buffalo hides hanging on the sides, he was sure. He also knew how sacred the buffalo were to the Indians. That alone would be a reason for the Indians to kill these men. "Grandfather scouted around the wagons and in the nearby woods, but couldn't find any trace of Captain Beall or the others. He felt the Indians had no doubt taken them alive to their campground and had made sport of their deaths. So you see, after

Beall and his friends spent the night with my grandfather, he never saw them alive again!”

I was fascinated by what Uncle Nell knew. “It's so exciting Uncle Nell,” I said. “I lived in the Harshbarger-Munger house, the same house where Captain Beall and his friends visited when your grandfather lived there,” I wanted to know more. “Do you know anything else about the house?”

“The house had been built on what was the original land grant given to a Mr. Mark Evans and later became part of the old Luck Farm Lands,” Uncle Nell began. “The old house had been built like a fortress with two stories, a basement, and an attic. Because of the threat of Indian attacks, the men in the family -- two at a time, would take turns on watch duty. They would lie on the attic floor at either end of the house where from the small windows on either side of the chimneys they could see for miles. This helped to give them early warning of an Indian attack.

“During the time my grandfather and his family lived in the house, it had been used as a stagecoach stopover. One of the stagecoach lines was owned and operated by the Bufords. When the stagecoach crossed Read Mountain, the driver would blow loudly on an elk horn. He would blow once for each traveler. That way, his grandfather would know how many guests to expect and how much food to prepare.”

Uncle Nell seemed to enjoy telling me stories, so I encouraged him to go on.

“Late one evening,” he began the next adventure, “just before dark, two men on horseback stopped at the old house hoping to find a place to stay the night. They were given a room on the second floor, and before going to bed that night, they asked my grandfather to wake them early the next morning. The next morning, grandfather called to the two men from the bottom of the stairs. The men didn't respond! Grandfather went up to the room and knocked loudly on the door. When there was still no response, he opened the door and entered the room. He found only one of the men -- lying on the bed; dead! The other man was gone. Grandfather examined the body for signs of what might have caused his death; nothing was found! Grandfather decided to bury the man." Uncle Nell stopped for a moment as if trying to figure out how he explains what he was about to say. "The strangest thing about all this was when grandfather had lived in the house, there was only one entrance. Because of Indian attacks, he was a very light sleeper. He was sure he didn't see or hear anything that night and could never understand how anyone could have gotten past him."

I was so happy after Uncle Nell told me this story. Now I know the spiritual revelations I had experienced on that winter day in the old house were real! But now I too had more questions about the murder. I now understood why on that summer day after Uncle Nell saw me in the field, he didn't want to discuss Mr. Brugh's unmarked grave.

Uncle Nell was always willing to tell me stories, and on another lazy afternoon, I decided to ask him about the name "Harshbarger-Munger."

He said the name came in part from the families that had lived in the house. "The Munger family and also Samuel and Isaac Harshbarger and his family. They'd lived in the house during the years when slavery in the South was an issue. It's been said he was a kind and generous man who hated the institution of slavery. He cared for the often sick and injured runaway slaves who were fortunate enough to make it to his home." Then Uncle Nell said something that startled me. He told me Harshbarger created a tunnel in one of the stone walls in the kitchen. He said Harshbarger left a few stones loose so they could be easily removed when they needed to open the tunnel.

I looked confused, and Uncle Nell said, "Oh, I guess when you lived there it was the basement."

I just nodded as Uncle Nell continued the story.

"When the slaves were in jeopardy of being found, Harshbarger would remove the loose stones and open the tunnel. The slaves would hide there until the soldiers left. Samuel Harshbarger was very good to the slaves. Many of them didn't have shoes, and by the time they reached his home, their feet were swollen, cut, and bleeding. Once after twelve or fifteen slaves had made it to Mr. Harshbarger's home, he was so touched he gave them all shoes and clothing for their long journey north — to their freedom.

"The Harshbarger's home was the last stop on what was called the 'Underground Railroad' before reaching The Black Horse Tavern. The tavern, located near the Hollins Railroad Station, probably about 6 miles away, was where the slaves could catch the train north to a free state.

After listening to his story, I realized, without even knowing it, that I had heard about Mr. Harshbarger before. "Uncle Nell does Mr. Harshbarger have anything to do with Hershberger Road?" I asked.

"Yes," he replied, "you're exactly right. Hershberger Road was named in honor of Samuel Harshbarger. That road was once the old trail that led to Salem, Virginia. In my grandfather's day, Salem was a day's travel from the old Harshbarger-Munger House. As I told you, Indian attacks were so frequent that the lands around the trail were barren. That land was called the "Badlands."

"So, Uncle Nell, what happened to Mr. Harshbarger?"

"Well, as far as I know, he eventually moved somewhere out

West.”

# CHAPTER ELEVEN
## Meeting The Lee Family

In 1947, Mr. and Mrs. Lee moved into the old Harshbarger-Munger House. My family was still living across the road with Uncle Nell.

One day, I decided to visit Mrs. Lee. It was strange to be in the house and not live there. Mrs. Lee was a very nice lady in her 40s. She had light brown hair and smiled as she said she was very happy to have me visit. When I explained that my family had lived in the house, she got all excited and told me she had just found Thomas Jefferson Beall's Bible in the attic. Just being in the house again made me feel that connection to my visions. I was hoping to find out more from Mrs. Lee, so I shared my story about finding the bible. "When I told my mother about the bible she said it didn't belong to me and made me put it back in the attic." I debated about telling Mrs. Lee about copying the letter, but then she surprised me.

"Then I have your mother to thank," Mrs. Lee said as she brought out the bible. "If it weren't for her instructing you to return it to the attic, I would never have found it there."

I couldn't wait to see if the letter and map were still inside and asked, "Can I hold it?"

Mrs. Lee handed me the bible as if it were a baby. "Now you be very careful. Since the covers of Beall's Bible are missing, I've decided to have my son-in-law make a wooden case with a lock to protect the bible."

I held the bible in my hands, and it felt the same as the day in the attic when I first found it. I turned the pages looking for the contents.

Mrs. Lee watched me and then asked, "Is this what you're looking for?" She held the letter and the map.

"Yes, oh yes!"

We talked for hours, trying to figure out what it all meant. We both believed it had some unknown value; however, we agreed if we were ever to learn of its intended use and importance, it would be years into the future.

I never told her I copied the letter or where it was hidden in the house. Sometime later, Mrs. Lee moved away.

# CHAPTER TWELVE
## Spirit Beckons Me To Follow

One beautiful spring day in 1950, a friend of mine, James Ellis, invited me to go fishing along the banks of the James River. He found us a nice sandbar along the bank, and we placed several fishing lines into the water. The fish were biting, so we stayed there.

I began to feel very strange when the same spirit I had come to recognize from the Old Harshbarger-Munger House appeared. The spirit beckoned me to follow it on a nearby path that led into Purgatory Mountain, in Buchanan, Virginia. I felt there was something I was supposed to see, and I was compelled to follow. I got up to go, but realized I had to explain this to James.

"I need to go—the spirit wants me to see something!"

"I don't know about this spirit, but I don't want you to go—and I certainly don't want to go with you," James said adamantly.

I was so torn—I wanted to follow the spirit, but in the end, I decided to stay with James.

"Let's go find another place to fish!" He didn't wait for me to answer. He just picked up the poles, and we left.

We found a place to fish, and eventually, I forgot about the spirit. The fishing here was good, so we stayed until late. When it began to get dark, another couple near us built a fire and invited us to join them. They introduced themselves as Robert and Mildred Henegar Robinson. We talked and talked and got friendly.

# CHAPTER THIRTEEN

## Planter's House

In October 1955, I had decided to take a vacation. My family was reluctant about my traveling alone and said I could go if I had a companion. I had heard so much about Reno, Nevada; how it was a twenty-four-seven town, with everything open around the clock. It sounded so exciting I knew that was the only place I wanted to go.

My friend Mark agreed to go with me. We were traveling by Greyhound Bus from Virginia to Nevada. Around midnight on Sunday night, we arrived in St. Louis, Missouri. The bus stopped to let some passengers off, and I was overcome with a feeling of tiredness. I just had to get off the bus and find a place to rest!

The bus driver helped us off, and Mark gathered our things. I went over to the bus driver and asked if he knew of a hotel nearby. I turned to look for Mark, and I heard, "Yes, you're in luck—just across the street." We crossed the street to where I believed the hotel was. It was a large building constructed of gray stone. We walked up to the double glass doors, and I gave them a shove and stepped forward. "What the...!" I exclaimed as I ran straight into the glass—the doors hadn't opened. In fact, they were locked.

"Are you all right?" Mark asked. I nodded while I caught my breath and finally said, "Yes. But what kind of hotel would keep its doors locked?" Mark and I just looked at each other.

I peeked through the glass and saw what appeared to be some sort of lobby. There was a framed portrait hanging on the wall. Moving back from the doors, I looked above the door. The sign read, "The Cotton Belt Building." To the right and adjacent to this name, I saw the name "Planter's House." The door had a square glass panel on its upper half and on the lower half, an "X" was carved into the wood. To the right, I saw a building constructed of dark wood. I walked over to the wooden door. This time I checked more carefully before attempting to open the door. I looked through the glass panel in the door and saw a lighted room. I motioned to Mark, "This must be the hotel." I turned the doorknob, and we entered the lobby of the Planter's House. We were amazed when we walked into the lobby. The floor was covered with thick, plush red carpet, and the walls were finished in a beautiful dark wood paneling. A large archway to the right of the front door formed the entrance to the octagon-shaped dining room, which was lighted with crystal chandeliers. As I walked past the dining room, I saw that all the guests were dressed in formal clothes. The ladies wore beautiful long dresses, and the men were all dressed in dark suits. The waiters also wore dark suits, but with long tails. They were serving the dining guests from gleaming brass serving carts. It was an elegant atmosphere indeed.

Mark and I walked over to the clerk's desk located in the right corner at the far end of the lobby. The clerk was a small man who appeared to weigh about 140 pounds and stood about five feet tall. He had a dark complexion, brown eyes, and black wavy hair. He was dressed in a dark suit, white shirt, and dark tie. As we approached, the clerk greeted us with a friendly and courteous smile and asked, "May I help you, miss?"

I replied, "Yes, we need accommodations."

His response seemed quite strange to us. "It's been some time since we've had visitors," he stated. "It will take the maid a few minutes to get the rooms ready."

The clerk reached under the countertop and lifted out a long, black, narrow register. He flipped through the pages from front to back, but all the pages were covered with names. He continued to search for a place for us to sign. In the middle of the register, he found some blank pages. When he turned the register around to face us, I was filled with an unexplainable impulse to flee. I immediately moved to the other end of his desk. I didn't say anything, but Mark must have seen something in my eyes. He signed the hotel register for both of us. Feeling relieved, I looked up, and my eyes were drawn to the wall near the clerk's desk. Hanging there was a portrait of a distinguished-looking middle-aged man with graying hair and blue eyes. He was clean-shaven. The man appeared to be heavy-set and was wearing a gray vested suit. The frame around the portrait was wide, with a sculptured design worked into its golden tones. I let my eyes trace around the frame to the bottom where I saw a large brass nameplate that bore the name, "George Rader Brugh." I wondered, *Where have I seen this man before?* The name was so familiar.

As if the clerk read my mind, he said, "The painting is Mr. Brugh. He was from Virginia, too—a fine Virginia gentleman who was one of our early proprietors. Mr. Brugh has been with us for ten years and then some very important business back east demanded his time—he had to deliver a letter to someone. He never explained more, and he never returned. Eventually, we assumed he must have been killed by Indians."

The clerk then asked, "Do you have any valuables you'd like kept in our safe tonight? It's the best and safest in all the West!"

I thanked him and said, "No, the only thing I have of any value is my watch, and I sleep with it on my arm."

He asked me again as he extended his hand to take the watch, and repeated, "I will be glad to keep it in the safe for you!"

Again I refused.

Feeling hungry, I turned back toward the dining room. There were still so many people eating, I knew it would take a long time to be served. I decided I was more tired than I was hungry and just wanted to go to the room. "Do you have an alarm clock?" I asked the desk clerk.

"No," he replied, "but the maid will wake you at whatever time you wish."

"Please have her wake me no later than six o'clock. We have a bus to catch at seven."

We thanked him and walked from his desk to the pink-colored Otis elevator. I pushed the button and waited. A voice from behind me said, "May I help you Miss?"

I turned around to see the bellboy. "I'm sorry Miss," he continued, "the elevator is out of order. It hasn't worked since the fire. We'll have to take the stairs to the second floor."

That's *strange*, I thought. I saw no evidence of any fire. The bellboy picked up our luggage, and Mark and I followed him.

The second floor was designed as a long narrow corridor with doors to rooms on either side. At the far end of the corridor over an entrance door, I could see a small exit sign. The walls on this floor were light gray, and the ceiling was white and showed no effects from a fire. The bellboy sat my luggage on the floor beside the door of the room that was directly in front of the stairs. Using a key which hung from a large rusty-looking key ring, he made several unsuccessful attempts to open the door. Mark also tried but failed then handed the key ring back to the bellboy. While I was watching the two of them trying to unlock the door, I had a strange feeling that I'd been here before, yet I was sure I hadn't. I seemed to be picking up feelings from another room, and it had something to do with a framed letter hanging on the wall and the man who'd been in that room.

Finally, the bellboy was able to open the door. "You have the best room in the house," he told me as he put my luggage inside the room. "This was President Grant's room."

The room was small with only one window and a bathroom. The long drapes at the window flowed down to the carpet. The bed was full-size with a high oak headboard and a thick patchwork quilt. A dresser and mirror and a straight-back chair, all made of oak, were the only other pieces of furniture. There were no decorations or paintings hanging on the walls.

After checking into another nearby room, Mark said he was going downstairs to get a drink. I was too tired to eat or drink anything, so I went to bed and quickly fell asleep. Sometime during the night, I was awakened by noises in the corridor, but I must have fallen back to sleep because the next thing I knew, I was awakened by a knock on the door. I called out, "Come in."

A woman wearing a long white starched dress smiled at me, "Good morning. It's six o'clock." Without saying another word, she crossed to the window and pulled back each side of the dark green velvet drapes. She tied each side back with a long golden-color braided rope with long tassels. I suppose I was so tired the night before that I hadn't noticed how elegant the drapes were.

With the maid's back still turned to me, she said, "Oh, honey, I wish you could've seen how the townspeople cheered President Grant whenever he stayed here. This was his room, you know, and when he visited, we'd hang a large American flag out this very window in his honor. The people would shout and cheer until the president would raise the window and wave to them."

The maid came over to the bed and pointed to a large purple-colored spot. It looked like something had been spilled on the quilt. I hadn't noticed it last night. I sat up and started to get out of bed when she ordered, "Don't you move until I've cleaned up this mess." To my amazement, a large white cloth seemed to suddenly appear in her hands. I'm sure she didn't have the cloth in her hand a moment before. The maid rubbed in a back-and-forth motion, and the spot miraculously disappeared. She smiled at me and left the room.

After the maid left my room, I got up and dressed. Mark knocked on the door ready to leave. I gathered my belongings and put down a two-dollar tip for the maid. I looked around one more time and then told Mark I was ready to leave. He picked up my luggage, and we left. On our way out, I noticed the desk clerk was the same one who had checked us in. We were almost at the front entrance when I heard the clerk call out, "Hurry back."

I thought as I walked out the door, leaving the Planter's House, *I'm not planning on coming back.*

# CHAPTER FOURTEEN
## The Road To The Beall Papers

Mark and I hurried along down the street from the Planters House in St. Louis, Missouri, to the Greyhound Bus terminal. Our bus was leaving for Reno, Nevada, at seven o'clock. The long bus trip west was long and uneventful, but certainly worth it--Reno was everything I could've imagined and more! I contacted my family and told them I'd gotten a job at the world-famous Harrah's Club. I worked in the music room making change for customers who played the slot machines. My family didn't like my being there and wanted me to come home.

In December 1955, Mark and I reluctantly returned to my home in Virginia. Once back in Virginia, my life took on other responsibilities, such as being that of a wife to James and mother to my two wonderful children. It wasn't until 1964 that I thought again about the Planters House. I learned that the Roanoke City Library had a copy of a manuscript called, "The Beale Papers," written in 1952, by George L. Hart Sr. The past was definitely coming back to haunt me—but in this case, it was spurring me on—to get those papers. I obtained a copy and finally sat down to read the document. Hart made reference to Beall having visited "Planters House" in 1822. I couldn't believe it! I was at Planters House in October of 1955 on my way to Nevada. Could I have been drawn there? I continued to read. The manuscript further explained that Beall met a friend at Planters House and gave him a "key" that if needed would decipher his codes for locating the treasure vault.

I then recalled what the desk clerk at Planters Hotel had told me. *He said, Mr. Brugh, the man in the picture in the lobby, had to leave to deliver a very important letter to someone back East.*

Suddenly it hit me! Could there be a connection between these two men: Beall and Brugh. Was this very important letter Mr. Brugh had to deliver, in fact, the "key" to the Beall treasure codes? -- I hesitated, then read on. What I read enlightened me about Thomas Jefferson Beall. I believe the documents I'd found in the attic bible were to be used as a key to decipher the codes for finding Beall's treasure.

I now understood the importance of the letter and map which I'd found tucked away in his Bible in the attic of the old Harshbarger-Munger House, after it became our home in 1939.

By the time I'd finished reading Mr. Hart's document, I surmised that sometime after June 1832, Mr. Brugh decided his friend Beall wasn't coming back. As instructed, he started on his journey to deliver Beall's letter to Mr. Morriss in Lynchburg, Virginia. Mr. Brugh's death stopped him from being able to complete his mission for his friend, Mr. Beall. When I put the manuscript down, I had so many questions — more than ever before, but maybe I was getting some of the parts of the puzzle. I supposed that before going to bed that night, Brugh had put Beall's Bible with its contents: the letter and map, in the old Harshbarger-Munger House attic to keep them safe. He probably would have left everything there until he was ready to leave for the last leg of this journey to Lynchburg as Beall had instructed him! But then I thought, *what if Brugh was killed before he could safely hide the papers, and the killer was the one who put the bible with its papers in the attic, where they would be secretly hidden away—until the killer wanted to retrieve them.* I knew I could go on and on with suppositions, but regardless of who put Beall's Bible in the attic, it had been there in the old house, for a long time before 1943, when the spirit led me to find it.

# CHAPTER FIFTEEN
## Recovering The "Key" Letter

Over the years I had never tried to return to the old Harshbarger-Munger House to try and recover my copy of Beall's letter from the fireplace mantle where I had hidden it. Then I heard that the house was vacant. That was like a sign -- I knew I had to get into the house and retrieve the letter.

Mildred Robinson Huffman and I met again many years after we'd shared a campfire on the beach. I'd gone to work for Kenrose Manufacturing Company in 1951. Mildred had been working for them for a while. We couldn't believe the coincidence and decided it was fate. We became close friends, and as our relationship grew, I began to relate some of my psychic experiences to her. When I told her what Uncle Nell told me about Captain Beall, Mildred wanted me to talk to her brother. She said, "George has been looking for the Beall Treasures for years. He'd read about them in treasure magazines," she told me.

Halloween night, 1965, Mildred, her brother George Henegar, my husband James, and I went to the old Harshbarger-Munger house. James waited in the car while the rest of us went into the house. In the house, the light from the full moon beamed through the windows. It provided barely enough light to see our way through the large rooms. I took the lead and went to the stairs to the second floor. Holding tightly to the back of each other's sweatshirts, we slowly ascended the staircase. I went straight to the bedroom which contained the fireplace where I'd hidden my copy of Beall's letter.

George pulled the mantle from the wall. There was nothing there! We searched in and around the fireplace, but still found nothing. I was so disappointed. We turned to leave when the same spirit presence I had experienced as a child living in this house entered the room. I could hear the spirit in my mind, "The last people who lived in the old house have your letter."

I told Mildred and George what the spirit had told me. They confessed they too, felt a presence, but neither one of them received any messages. "My letter's not here," I said. We may as well leave."

We left, but in the hallway Mildred said she wanted to go to another room. She pointed to the door and I explained, "When I'd lived there, that room had been unfinished and I had played there."

The door was secured with a padlock. Mildred and George both pulled at the lock, but it would not come loose. I gave it a try, but couldn't unlock the door. We headed back downstairs when I again felt the same spiritual presence.

The spirit was in the next room and mentally communicated with me. "Come back upstairs. I have something to show you." I told Mildred and George, and they agreed if I was going back upstairs, they would go with me.

George reached the top of the stairs first, and I could feel the spirit between us. George jumped into a corner of the room. I stumbled on the stairs—but luckily for me Mildred was behind me. Standing on the staircase, the light from the moon shone in such a way, I was able to see into the same unfinished room which had only moments before been padlocked. Suddenly a black cloud filled the doorway. George was stunned and shouted, "Mildred, can you see Claudine?"

"Yes, she's standing in front of me on the stairs."

"Can you see into the room?" George asked

"Yes why?" Mildred answered

"Just hold onto Claudine and don't let go--no matter what happens!"

I knew then that George must have seen the same black cloud. I had heard every word between George and Mildred, but I was too deep in concentration to join the conversation. I sensed a different spiritual presence within the black cloud. That spirit moved directly in front of me. It was so close I could feel my hair stand on end.

The intensity of the moment mounted. I sensed this spirit was desperately trying to tell me something, only it could not. "Oh my God!" I exclaimed out loud. "What is it trying to tell me?" Then suddenly that barrier was gone. The spirit mentally communicated, "Your neck -- your neck-- your neck!" It then repeated those same words -- each time, I could feel the intensity of the statement. By the third time I threw my hands up and clutched my neck. I felt very vulnerable. I didn't know what to expect next -- I felt a need to protect my neck. *Spirit, what do you want with my neck? Do you want to choke me? I needed to know what this black spirit was going to do to me.*

Still clutching my neck, the answer came to me. The spirit wanted me to recall the day back in the nineteen-forties when I was being led to the attic. *Yes, I passed through this very same room on my way to the attic. Oh my goodness! That was the day I'd seen the ornate necklace around my neck in the mirror on the dresser.* The spirit in the black cloud moved to the west bedroom where I believed Mr. Brugh had met his death. Suddenly it was gone!

With the cloud gone, George joined Mildred and me on the stairs, and we descended to the first floor. We walked to the kitchen and out the door. George was about to close the door behind us when the doorknob started turning back and forth—by itself! George jumped back and bumped into Mildred and me. I told them to go to the car and I went over to the door and closed it.

My husband James was waiting patiently in the car, "So what happened?" he asked as we got in.

But before we could answer, we all saw a ball of fire shoot out of a window on the second floor of the old house. It came from the room where I believe Mr. Brugh was murdered. With lightning speed it raced toward Read Mountain!

The following week, I started my search for the last family who had lived in the old house. I was sure they had to have taken my copy of Captain Beall's letter from the fireplace. I talked with the nearby neighbors, but none of them had been acquainted with the family or were even sure of their name. I finally decided to let the matter rest. I felt if it were intended for me to find them, then one day I would.

# CHAPTER SIXTEEN
## Led To The "Key"

Following the night Mildred, George, and I visited the old house, I went on with my life without further pursuit of the Beall Letter. Five years had passed when one Sunday morning in 1969, upon waking, I realized that before 11:00 a.m. I would stand in the presence of the family who had taken my letter from its hiding place.

During breakfast, I explained to my husband James what I was feeling and asked him to drive me to the old Harshbarger-Munger House on Hershberger Road.

When we approached the house, I had a feeling that we should keep going. "Didn't you want to come to the house?" James asked. He was puzzled, but no more than I was. I just had to go with my instincts. I directed James to drive several more miles. When we drove past old Mountain Road, I strongly sensed that someone living there knew something of importance to me. He continued to drive slowly until I knew which house I was looking for. When I saw it, I asked him to stop the car.

The name on the mailbox was "Hale." James waited in the car. I went up to the door and knocked. A petite, gray-haired lady opened the door.

"Good morning." I said. "Are you Mrs. Hale?"

"Yes," she replied, "I am. How can I help you?"

I told her I was trying to locate a family who had lived on East Hershberger Road in the early sixties, in a house that used to be called the "Harshbarger-Munger House."

"Oh, yes," she smiled, I know the people you're looking for. Their name is Journell. Eula Journell is a friend of mine."

Mrs. Hale invited me into her home. "Come on in; I'll give her a call. You can talk to her yourself." She telephoned Mrs. Journell and then put me on the phone.

I spoke to Mrs. Journell for a few minutes and then she invited me to visit her at her home and gave me the directions. I thanked Mrs. Hale and then joined James in the car. I told him what happened and gave him the directions. James drove to the address on Dale Avenue, S.E., in Roanoke, where Mrs. Journell had told me she lived with her daughter.

Mrs. Journell opened the door and welcomed me into her home. The first thing I noticed was a large clock hanging on the wall in the living room. The time was a few minutes before 11:00 a.m.

Mrs. Journell motioned for me to sit down and introduced her son, Elwood. I explained to them about living in the same house on Hershberger Road as they did. I told them I had found a letter and a map tucked away in an old Bible in the old house. I explained that I had made a copy and had hidden the letter behind the fireplace mantle in the west bedroom on the second floor. I described the location of the room to them and the letter that I had copied. I told them that I had left the letter unsigned and had folded a white blank sheet of paper around my letter before enclosing it in a white personal size envelope. After sealing the envelope, I wrote the word 'IMPORTANT' in large letters on the front of the envelope. Then I described how I had slipped the envelope between the mantle and the wall on the right side of the mantle where there was a slight separation. During this time Mrs. Journell and her son had not said a word.

"Did you find my letter," I anxiously asked.

Elwood turned to his mother and said, "Mom, you know that no one else in the world could have told us this about that letter except the person who put it there.

Mrs. Journell smiled and said, "Yes, Elwood and I had found the letter. One day when I was cleaning in that room and dusting the fireplace mantle, I noticed a piece of white paper sticking out between two loose bricks on the right side of the fireplace. I called to Elwood to help me. He used his pocketknife to pry the bricks out, and the letter fell out onto the floor. The word "IMPORTANT" on the envelope stopped me from just discarding it."

Mrs. Journell stopped, looked at Elwood, and hesitated. I wasn't sure she was going to tell me anything more. "Please Mrs. Journell," I pleaded. That letter is very valuable, and I now know what I need to do with it. You see, the letter you recovered from the fireplace mantle was a copy of a letter signed by Thomas Jefferson Beall. Captain Beall was involved with a buried treasure—one believed to be very valuable! The letter I copied was the key to codes that would lead to the treasure."

Mrs. Journell nodded, "I no longer have your letter. I wasn't sure what to do with it, so I showed it to another son, Ernest. He thought we should take the letter to Hollins College."

*Hollins College,* I thought, that's only a few miles away. I was definitely getting closer to finding my letter.

"As I recall, it was raining that day," Mrs. Journell continued. "We drove to Hollins by way of Route 11, and I stayed in the car while Ernest and Elwood went into the college. It wasn't that long before they returned. They told me they'd talked to a history professor, Dr. Carl Ramsey. After examining the letter, Dr. Ramsey told them he had a friend in Washington, D.C., who was a computer expert. He said his friend knew how to chemically treat the faded letters to make them legible. Ramsey wanted permission to send the letter to him. The boys gave their okay." Then Mrs. Journell paused. This time she didn't want to look at me. "I'm sorry Claudine; he never returned the letter."

# CHAPTER SEVENTEEN
## The Search For The "Key" Ends

After talking with Mrs. Journell and her son Elwood, I knew the next step was to track down Dr. Ramsey. I called Hollins College, and they told me, "Dr. Ramsey is no longer at Hollins. He'd moved to Boone, North Carolina, and had taken a teaching position at Appalachian College. *I hoped one more call would lead to my letter.*

I dialed the number the girl at Hollins College had given me, and for a moment I felt uneasy—but that passed when the operator answered, "Appalachian College."

"I'd like to speak with Dr. Ramsey," I said, trying to remain calm.

"Oh, I'm so sorry to have to tell you, Dr. Ramsey had died in a car accident," the operator said.

I lost my breath for a moment and then asked, "Do you happen to have a telephone number for Dr. Ramsey's next-of-kin?"

"Yes, of course, just hold a moment while I get it for you."

The silence on the phone was only overshadowed by the loud screams in my head. *I had come so close — and now…*

The woman came back on the line and gave me a telephone number for Dr. Ramsey's father. I thanked her and hung up.

I sat looking at the number. *Was this going to be the call that gives me my answers or be just another dead end?* I couldn't keep speculating. I picked up the phone and dialed the number.

"I'm sorry. I'd not seen any such letter as you describe in my son's personal belongings," the elder Mr. Ramsey said.

I was so disappointed, but I needed to try to find out whatever I could. I explained what Mrs. Journell said about Dr. Ramsey sending my letter to his friend in Washington, D.C., "Maybe you know who that would be?" I held my breath.

"My son had many respected colleagues all over the world. I am sorry — I have no idea who he might have been referring to."

"I don't mean to take up your time Mr. Ramsey, but could you think again—Elwood Journell thought your son's friend in Washington D.C. held a degree in computer science."

Mr. Ramsey paused, and then said in an apologetic-sounding tone, "I wish I could help you, but I can't. I wish you good luck in finding your letter. Goodbye."

"Thank you again for speaking with me. Goodbye." My heart dropped as I hung up the phone. How could all the clues have led me so far — only to come to this? I know there's something I'm supposed to find out—and someday I Will!

# CHAPTER EIGHTEEN
## The Blue Ridge Parkway Incident

After my unsuccessful search for my copy of Beall's letter, I had let my desire to find the letter go. I went on with my life. I was recovering from a surgical procedure I had undergone three months earlier. When I felt the need to get out of the house, I decided to go for a short drive. Something led me to drive north toward the Blue Ridge Parkway. The road led to the little town of Buchanan, and the James River.

I parked the car alongside the road. The temperature was extremely hot for that time of year, but a cool breeze from the mountains felt so refreshing, I got out of my car. I saw an old-looking oak tree a short distance away. I walked over to the tree; it was so peaceful and quiet. I sat in the shade of the trees, enjoying the cool breeze and listening to some birds chirping in the branches above.

Nearby, I saw a trail road. As I concentrated on the trail, I felt the presence of the same spiritual entity that had visited me in the past. It was beckoning me again to follow. I sensed the spirit wanted to show me something. I eased myself up and envisioned Captain Beall and two men making their way out West for the third time. I could feel the men's anxiousness to get back to the gold mines they'd discovered. Then the spirit mentally communicated to me a sense of where the trail road led. I felt a cold chill of death! I wanted to follow the spirit and learn more, but I was still weak from my recent surgery. I had to realize I could not go where those answers were. The spirit seemed to understand my feelings, for it departed as quickly as it had appeared.

I sat back down under the tree and caught my breath. I felt a new awareness and connection to this place. Then my thoughts carried me back to 1947. Uncle Nell had told me about the disappearance of Captain Beall and the other two men and how Uncle Nell's grandfather was the one who'd found his best friend Beall's abandoned wagons near the James River. I felt very sure that I must have been near where they had been killed by the Indians.

# CHAPTER NINETEEN
## Visions Of The Treasure Vault

During the late 1960s, my husband James and I would often go hiking in the Blue Ridge Mountain range, in Bedford County, Virginia, with our friends George Henegar and his sister, Mildred Robinson. George had helped build the old Civilian Conservation Corp Roads through the areas of the mountain I was interested in. We would often talk about those trails, and he was a great asset in my search for information about the original trails.

When we would hike passed certain areas along the trail, I would feel a definite pulling sensation, but then it would be gone.

One night I had a vivid dream that I was standing on the trail, and walking toward me was a tall man. I couldn't make out his features, but he was dressed in buckskin clothing and wore a fur cap. The man walked up to me and asked, "Do you want to know where I buried my treasure?"

"Yes," I replied.

He placed his hands ever so gently on my shoulders and turned me in the opposite direction. "Go as straight as you can," he told me. "You will find the place where I buried my treasure."

I woke with a start and realized. It was Captain Beall who spoke to me!

I told James about my dream, and he decided to go with me to the trail to search for the treasure vault.

When we reached the same area along the trail as I remembered from my dream, I closed my eyes. I instinctively turned in the direction the man in the buckskin clothing showed me. When I opened my eyes, there before me stood a mountain and the place I was being led to. I told James to look up—for that was where I had to go!

"Do you intend to climb this mountain?" he asked. "I have to tell you that I think that's a really foolish idea. Just look," he said pointing to the terrain, "trees, briar patches, and large stones are all in your way."

"I hear what you're saying James, but I'm going anyway!"

"Okay then, you just be careful," I heard him say as I started my climb.

Every time I encountered an obstacle, I would go around it and continue climbing. Finally, I saw it. This was the same formation I'd seen in my vision as a child at the old Harshbarger-Munger House. This was the place the spirit had described to me. "There is also another place in a distant mountain. When you stand before that place, you will know it for there is no other place like it in all of the mountains." Yes, this stone formation was just as the spirit had described it.

# CHAPTER TWENTY
## Visions Of A Second Vault

The climb down the mountain was disheartening. I had believed that once I stood at the site the spirit had showed me as a child, all my questions would be answered—but now all I had were more questions. Why had the spirit shown me this spot when there was nothing there? I had searched and searched — but by the time I headed back down the mountain I was sure, if there was any treasure there — it wasn't there now.

Several months later, I had another dream. I dreamed I was standing near the stone vault when I noticed a middle-aged woman standing near a log cabin. I walked toward her, "I am glad you came," she said. "I want to show you where something is buried."

The next weekend my husband James went with me to the area I had seen in my dream. I scouted looking for the log cabin, while he sat on the ground. I noticed a mound about waist high that was covered with weeds and bushes. I kicked about the mound with my boots and uncovered some stones. A closer look suggested the stones were once part of a chimney. I kicked around some more and discovered the foundation of an old log cabin. I bent down to examine the site further when the spirit appeared to me again, just as it had so many times before. I could feel it beckoning me to follow it, and this time I did.

Not far from where the old log cabin had once stood, the spirit showed me a small pond that led to the entrance of what appeared to be andm mining shaft that had been sealed up with stones. I looked closely at the large stones. They'd obviously been placed there long ago. The spirit communicated to me that the largest stone should be moved first.

The stone was just too large for me to move. I sat down on the ground. Once again, I've come so far for answers and I had to accept that I wouldn't get my answers — not yet. I was feeling down when I realized this experience wasn't for nothing -- I learned about a second possible treasure vault! I started to think, what is the spirit trying to tell me with this vision — *maybe the second vault means the pots of gold were moved from the original place Captain Beall buried them, to here!*

I rushed back to where James was waiting and told him about the second treasure vault. He agreed, if we could find a way to move those stones, we'd come back and see if the treasure is there!

# CHAPTER TWENTY-ONE
## My Return To The Childhood Scene

By the 1970s, Locust Level, the brick building at the edge of Buford's airfield was owned by Mr. and Mrs. J.T. Howell. It was their place of residence, and they operated an antique shop at the same location.

I had a feeling; I just wanted to go back and see — if I went inside... My niece Barbara Smith had known about my story regarding the Beall treasure and my early childhood experiences at Locust Level. She agreed to go with me.

This was the first time I'd been at Buford's airfield since the day in 1938 when as a child I had the vision of my mother on the back porch.

Mrs. Howell greeted us and showed us her beautiful collection of antique glassware on display in the shop area. As soon as we entered the shop I felt like a powerful bolt of lightning danced beside me! I became excited, my heart began to pound, and I was filled with energy. "Oh my God, Barbara!" I blurted out, "This is the back porch I told you about!"

My statement shocked Mrs. Howell. "Yes," she indicated, "You're right—this area where you're standing was once the back porch." She continued to explain, "After the Civil War, the Henry Buford house was joined to Locust Level, It had once been called "Lee Hall," in honor of General Robert E. Lee, a friend of Captain Paschal Buford.

As I looked around the room, I noticed an area high on the wall just in front of where we were standing. "Look," I said pointing out the area, "you can still see where the upper balcony was attached to the back porch."

Mrs. Howell graciously offered to show us the rest of the house. In the front of the house, there was a steep staircase that led to the second floor. When I put my right hand on the banister I felt a shocking revelation! People and things from a much earlier time period flooded my mind. "Oh, Mrs. Howell," I asked as we climbed the stairs, "is there a little playroom at the top of the stairs, and are the little wooden toys still on the shelves on the left wall and from the window, you can see Route 460?"

"Well," she stammered, obviously stunned by my question, "there is a little room, but I don't know if it was ever a playroom."

I moved passed Mrs. Howell and could feel a gentle touch on my back — as if someone's hands were on my back. I felt as though I was a little child again, and then I felt the presence of a woman who seemed to have once been my mother.

When I reached the top of the stairs, I ran directly to the room I was sure was the little playroom. Barbara and Mrs. Howell followed. Everything in this room felt familiar. I had a clear sense of a time long ago when I'd played in this little place for hours at a time. I knew the little wooden toys were neatly placed on the shelves on the left wall! And I was sure; from the window, I could see Route 460. I went to the window and looked out. I not only saw Route 460, but the old dirt trail roads that had come into the yard of Locust Level many years ago; long before Route 460 existed. I remembered standing in front of this window! I envisioned that I was waiting for a man riding a white horse to come down the dirt trail road. I could remember the feelings of joy I had when I first spotted him. I ran from the window shouting to everyone in the household that he'd arrived! Still gazing out of the window, I could again feel the lonely pain I felt when he didn't come. I now believed this man was someone close to me; like a father or grandfather.

Barbara and Mrs. Howell joined me in the little room. Barbara was surprised by the accuracy of my description. I led them out into the hallway and stood in the doorway of another room. We didn't enter this room, but when I looked, I could hear the voices of my grandparents saying goodnight to me - I felt my mother again!

I walked across the hall to another bedroom. When I entered I was immediately drawn to a massive bed with a high headboard and bedposts topped with large wooden cannonballs constructed into the headboard. I had a sense that the cannonball on the right side of the bed had never been glued into place and that it held a secret compartment! "Oh, Barbara!" I exclaimed, "I wonder if after all this time anyone has fixed that loose cannon ball?" I reached out and lifted it from its bedpost.

Standing in the doorway, Mrs. Howell was shaken, "I had no idea!" she said.

I then lifted the antique white bed cover that flowed to the floor and was adorned with fringes. Through the fringes, I could see marks cut into the bedrail. The marks appeared to be in groups of six or sevens. I felt that long ago these marks were made to count off time. I didn't know why.

I pulled the bed cover back to better observe the cut marks and I envisioned a little girl lying in the bed. She appeared to be asleep. Her beautiful long flaxen blond hair was parted in the middle and framed her small face. She looked to be about five years old. Before I could think about who she might be and why I was seeing an apparition of her, I felt the entire room swell with a sensation of grief and pain - as one feels at the time of a death or the loss of a loved one.

In my mind I heard the screams and wails of a young woman deep in the throes of grief. The sounds were a deafening wave of silence that death brings with it. I turned from the bed and ran from the grief-stricken room. I saw that Mrs. Howell was nowhere to be seen. Barbara noticed how shaken I was and we returned to the first floor. We walked to a room at the front of the house. Barbara turned to see me standing very still. "Deanie, are you all right?" she asked.

"No." I replied. "Someone from my past is calling to me - telling me I cannot play in this room! That I will only mess it up!"

Barbara grabbed my arm and pulled me into the room. I felt very uncomfortable as if I were disobeying someone's orders. I quickly left and Barbara followed.

Barbara and I then went to the east room, which Mrs. Howell told us was once called the parlor room. I immediately recalled that I started to connect with my very first supernatural experience here on the site of Buford's Airport in 1938. I was drawn to the large colonial-style window on the opposite wall. I looked out on what remained of the Buford's airfield landing strip.

An almost overwhelming, electrifying sensation moved over my entire body! I knew I had to look down; just in front of me. I was almost afraid to look, but I forced my gaze downward. I was shocked at what my eyes beheld!

My mind flooded with questions. Was something actually there, or was it just a vision? I saw an old antique doll lying in an antique carriage. I was so shaken. I reached for Barbara's arm to steady myself. I said, "Barbara, Barbara, look down in front of us and tell me if you see anything."

Barbara's reaction told me all I needed to know-the color had left her face and she could hardly speak! She composed herself and began to describe the doll and its dress. Then she concluded, "Deanie, it's your dress! It's like the one you said you could see yourself wearing that day, here at Buford's Airfield when you were with your father!"

"Tell me Barbara, please-just so I'm sure, what does it look like."

"There's a square neckline in front: full puffed sleeves just above the elbows, and a blue satin ribbon encircling the waistline. Also a bow tied in the front with ribbons streaming down either side almost touching the hemline of the dress. Go on Deanie, pick up the doll and hold her."

"I want to -- I just can't!"

"Why? Don't you think you should pick her up?" Barbara tried to encourage me.

"I just can't." I didn't tell Barbara I was afraid that from somewhere deep in my soul memories would surface that I wasn't sure I could deal with. "I just want to go!" was all I said. As we left the room, I knew I had to leave without ever touching the golden-haired doll.

Mrs. Howell had been on the telephone when Barbara and I first entered the store area. I asked her about the doll in the carriage. She said the doll and carriage, along with the cannonball poster bed upstairs, had come with the estate." She emphasized, they were never to be sold apart from the estate. Other than that she didn't know anything more about those specific items. "I can tell you that my husband and I purchased the property from the last Bufords that lived here." Mrs. Howell continued, "The Buford's had one daughter, Kitty Buford Pendleton, but after the death of James Buford, his wife had decided to sell."

I had thought that was all Mrs. Howell could tell us, but she added, "Oh this may interest you. After having lived at Buford's Tavern for several years, late one night after my husband and I had went to bed, we heard footsteps. They sounded like they were coming from the front hallway. We'd always felt some type of presence in the house, but we'd never seen anything until that night. The footsteps continued to our bedroom and a man dressed in dark clothes and wearing a large, dark-brimmed hat walked over to the foot of our bed. He looked at us a few minutes then went out the door."

We thanked Mrs. Howell and started to leave. I was stopped by a presence standing at the top of the stairway. It wanted me to come back upstairs - something to do with what he had left behind. I was drained from all that had happened already that day - that I just couldn't! I heard the words in my mind, *"No, not today ---- maybe another day."* The spirit seemed to understand.

When we were about to leave, I noticed a small brick and wood building in the backyard. It felt so familiar; like a kitchen from long ago and someone giving me cookies --

# CHAPTER TWENTY-TWO
## The Painting

I had thought a great deal about what Mrs. Howell had said and decided to find Kitty Buford Pendleton. My friend Dawn Hale and I met with Mrs. Pendleton. Kitty told us she'd been the last Buford descendant to have been born at the Locust Level house in Montvale, Virginia. "I loved to explore the vast terrain and run through the open fields along Goose Creek. Sometimes I'd find an Indian arrowhead and it felt like finding 'a little jewel worth the search,' she said.

"Did you ever play in the parlor room?" I asked.

"Truthfully there was something very uncomfortable about the old house. So I tried to be outdoors whenever possible." She tried to change the subject, "Did you know that Locust Level had a family cemetery?" She didn't wait for an answer. "I loved to spend time there-where my kin, lay asleep beneath the sod."

Kitty got up, "There's something I want to show you." She held an old newspaper picture of herself and her father. Kitty was seated on her father's plane at Buford's Airport. The picture reminded me of my plane ride with my father and Mr. Buford back in 1938.

Before leaving, Kitty went upstairs and returned with an old oil painting. "The painting has always been in our family." Kitty said. "As far as I know it was painted by one of the early Bufords who'd lived at Locust Level."

"It's very interesting. Do you know the history?" *I was interested in the dirt trail road that crossed the yard.*

"The painting depicts several early Buford homes which surround Locust Level, that were built by Captain Paschal Buford in 1820. The dirt trail roads are "the old colonial trails, what would now be Route 460. The trails wind their way down from a distant knoll into the front yard of Locust Level -- then fade into the distance."

The painting did show the old trail road! It reminded me of what I saw that day in 1970 when Barbara Smith and I visited Locust Level. When I looked out of the window from the playroom, in my vision I saw the exact trails depicted in the painting.

After seeing that painting I knew I had to go to Route 460 and look for the trail. I walked north of Buford's Tavern and found the trail, exactly where I expected it to be. I believe it was the same trail I saw in my vision in 1970; the same one in the painting.

# CHAPTER TWENTY-THREE
## Finding George Rader Brugh

After speaking with Kitty Pendelton, I felt I'd gotten as much information as possible about the Buford's and Locust Level. I turned my attentions to the Brugh family. I located a "Brugh" family living in the Mill Creek area of Botetourt County, Virginia. I called and explained to Mrs. Brugh that I was interested in learning more about one of the Brugh men who'd lived long ago. She was very gracious and I asked her if I could visit her and look at any family records that she might have. She told me she'd be glad to share what she had - their family records went back to the first Brugh's who'd come to this country from Germany.

My daughter Julia went with me to visit Mrs. Brugh that same day. Mrs. Brugh welcomed us into her home. I told her what I knew about George Rader Brugh and how he'd been the keeper of the key to the Beall Treasure. I also explained what I believed about his death. I told her I was determined not to give up my quest to prove that man was indeed George Rader Brugh. I wanted Mrs. Brugh to know how strongly I felt his story should be told and how happy I was to finally find some Brughs around who'd care enough to want to know about the death of one of their ancestors.

Mrs. Brugh had listened attentively; without saying a word. When I finished she got up and brought out two large loose-leaf notebooks that contained the family records. I put the files on my lap. I didn't have to look far to find the genealogy chart for George Rader Brugh. What I'd believed I knew about him was confirmed in these papers. Mr. Brugh had never married and his family had lost contact with him after he'd gone out west. Mrs. Brugh also had several photo albums that she allowed us to look through. I found one photo that I believed to have been George when he was a young man. I asked Mrs. Brugh if I could remove the photo so I could look at the back -- written there was his name, "George Rader Brugh." I wanted to make copies of the records, but Mrs. Brugh was unable to accompany me that day. "Please," she said getting up to escort us to the door, "come back again perhaps at a later date."

A few months later I again visited with Mrs. Brugh, hoping this time to make copies of the Brugh family records. Mrs. Brugh again brought out the records, but this time the genealogy chart for George Rader Brugh wasn't there. His photo was also missing. I brought this to Mrs. Brugh's attention and asked her if she knew where they were?

Mrs. Brugh told me she had the secretary from Mill Creek Baptist Church come over and redo the records. She explained that for safety sake, the records were now in a bank vault. I was so disappointed. I could only assume by her actions that she didn't want the Brugh name associated in any way with the Beall Treasure.

It wasn't until 1985 that I again tried to contact a Brugh. My brother-in-law William E. Brugh and my son-in-law William R. Ball went with me to talk with a Brugh family living in Salem, Virginia. My brother-in-law didn't know them as kin, but all his life he'd heard about the Beall Treasures and a possible Brugh family connection. William did tell me both he and George Rader Brugh were descendants of Hermanus Brugh, who was the patriarch of the Brugh family in the United States. "Hermanus," he said, "along with many other German people had migrated to America to escape invading forces in Germany over one hundred and fifty years ago. They'd settled in the foothills of the Blue Ridge Mountains of Virginia." He concluded by saying, "Today, many of Brugh's descendants are still living here."

This Brugh family we went to see in Salem, had a large genealogical chart of the Brugh family dating back to the early 1700's, which they allowed me to see.

I found the name George Brugh recorded for the period of time I believed he lived. This genealogical chart confirmed what I had seen when I went through Mrs. Brugh's records. I asked for permission to make a copy of this record - but the family denied my request. It seemed strange that no Brugh family member would allow me to make a copy of their family records to prove the identity of one George Rader Brugh.

I left the house of William Brugh and glanced around. I wasn't going to let the events leading to this day stop me.

# CHAPTER TWENTY FOUR

## The End Of A Journey--Or Just The Beginning

I continued my search to uncover information about Brugh, Beall, and what happened to them. I'd contacted the Chamber of Commerce in St. Louis, Missouri to learn more about Planter's House. In a courteous voice, the operator explained, "I'm sorry, but the hotel you're inquiring about was destroyed by a fire in 1887. The rebuilt Planter's House ceased to operate in 1922 at which time the stone building was sold and became known as the Cotton Belt Building."

In 1985, I decided to go back to the second vault that I'd visited in the sixties. Floodwaters had done considerable damage to the mountains and trail roads. The mudslides had been so devastating that nothing even remotely resembled the old cave or a mining shaft.

I had also located Mrs. Lee again. When I asked her about Beall's Bible, she didn't seem to know what I was talking about.

Exhausted, I opened my eyes and returned to the present. I sat very still. I couldn't stop thinking about Beall and Brugh and their connection. Finally, I concluded that Beall's Bible and my copy of his letter must be out there somewhere -- and when the time is right - I know they will surface. As far as George Rader Brugh, I still believe he was the dead man Uncle Nell indicated was buried in the field by the Harshbarger-Munger House.

I glanced at my watch and couldn't believe the time. I had to return to the needs of the day. I got up and then stood very still - a chill came over me. Perhaps one day the spirit will return - but until then, I know my quest will continue -- not for the gold, but for my desire to let the spirit of Mr. Brugh rest ... properly buried with his kin.

# AUTHOR'S SUMMATION

Since finishing this book, I've continued to search for information. In the "Virginia" section of The Richmond Times Dispatch, Sunday, October 3, 1993, staff writer, John Hoke wrote an article about the legendary Beall Treasure. Hoke interviewed Peter Veimeister of Bedford, Virginia, author of "The Beale Treasure: A History of a Mystery, and Joseph Duran, a Cheyenne Indian.

Here are those interviews:

"CHEYENNE MEMORY FUELS TREASURE QUEST
BUT CODE BREAKER CAN'T GO FOR GOLD UNTIL U.S. SAYS SO
By John Hoke
Times-Dispatch Staff Writer
Sunday, October 3, 1993
Edition: City, Section: Area/State, Page C-1
Dateline: MONTVALE

As a child at his Cheyenne grandfather's knee in Colorado, Joseph Duran was told a passed-through-the-generations tale of great treasure -- gold and silver taken from the Spaniards and hidden in the mountains of the East.

In the mid-1960s, Duran, now a computer technician in Michigan, happened across an Argosy magazine article about the famed Beale treasure - four tons of gold, silver and jewels hidden near the Peaks of Otter in the early 19th century with an unsolved numerical code holding specific directions to the lost riches.

"I read that account and all that my grandfather told me came back," Duran said. "My God, that is the same story." Consumed with breaking the ciphers and solving the mystery, Duran in the mid-1970s began making annual summer treks to Bedford to comb old records for clues.

He hooked up with dairy farmer Jimmy Luck, who grew up in Goose Creek Valley between the Peaks and Montvale and lived with the Beale legend all his life, often finding intrepid fortune hunters digging on his property. Luck gave Duran a place to stay, local insight, geographical references and historical perspective while Duran labored over the enigmatic puzzle.

In 1990, Duran said he cracked the code, using an obscure 174-year-old treaty between the United States and Spain as the key. The information he gleaned conflicted with much of the conventional wisdom about the treasure.

According to the code, the treasure, rather than being buried four miles from present-day Montvale, was hidden four miles from Buchanan -- on the north slope of the Blue Ridge and within sight of the James River. That would put it in Botetourt County rather than Bedford, as most Beale aficionados believed.

And rather than "buried in a vault," it was "buried in a fault" or cave, Duran said the codes told him.

Duran and Luck began scouring the thick woods on the Botetourt side of the Blue Ridge Parkway in the vicinity of Boblett's Gap. Duran found a cave that met the description in June 1990. The weight of an old tree had cracked an opening in some rocks.

About 70 feet away they found the original opening of the cave, impenetrable after a few dozen feet. But wedged into the roof of the cave were two pieces of old lumber, with a rusted handmade nail and a charred spot as if a lantern had hung there. An old iron stove front was found outside.

Duran and Luck were able to squeeze down the opening created by the old tree. Over a series of visits they explored the cave -- a precarious enterprise because of the loose rock.

Duran said he reached the end of the cave, where dirt had seeped down and effectively sealed it. Ancient-looking timbers had been wedged in to support the roof.

"It was incredible. I only had a flashlight. I was down that hole at the end of a 50-foot rope. The adrenalin was really going."

Duran thinks he was just a few feet from the legendary treasure.

He applied to the Jefferson National Forest-- the cave is on U.S. Forest Service land -- for permission to dig through the dirt to find what is on the other side.

Permission was granted in March 1992, when Duran and Luck and three forest rangers returned to the cave. Duran and Luck squeezed down the hole only to find that the sealed end was blocked by fallen rocks. The roof had caved in, and it was too dangerous to attempt further exploration.

Duran had to apply again for a permit, this time to bring in a backhoe.

He's still waiting, and suspicious of the government's delays. Last month, frustrated and virtually penniless, Duran, 58, returned to Michigan.

Though the Beale legend and the frequent claims of solving the riddle invite skepticism, Duran and Luck still have quite a tale.

Even Bill Baggett, a Jefferson Forest ranger who over 19 years has processed dozens of applications to dig for the treasure on federal lands, was impressed.

"Duran has about as good a case as anybody I've heard," Baggett said.

Others are less impressed, suggesting that the cave is actually an old mine that would have been dug after the treasure was supposedly buried. That theory would explain the presence of the support timbers.

The moss-rimmed cave, with a foul, warm breath emanating from the entrance, cuts into the side of the Blue Ridge. The 6 foot opening falls quickly into darkness.

Duran says the cave parallels the slope of the surface back about 65 feet, where he proposes to use a backhoe to dig down a few feet to where he believes the treasure waits.

The Forest Service is not intentionally delaying Duran, Baggett said, but his staff is overburdened with other work. The new permit has been put on a back burner because the land disturbance will require extensive environmental analysis under federal law.

"We just haven't gotten around to it," he said. "I feel for Duran. He has spent a whole lot of time and effort on it."

Baggett said he gets at least one or two applications from Beale treasure hunters a year. "A lot of them make a lot of sense. Some of them make hardly any."

The hundreds of Beale sleuths who search federal and state lands, with and without permission, are a virtual cottage industry for Bedford.

Peter Viemeister of Bedford, whose "The Beale Treasure: A History of a Mystery" is perhaps the definitive account, says the treasure seekers often try to act innocent at the county courthouses and museums in the area when asking for maps and records from around 1820. Furtive explorations by slow-moving cars with out-of-state plates are common.

"What makes it so consuming is it's like a lottery. It's worth a little work because even if it's a long shot, it has a big payoff," Viemeister said.

"Some only want to get the money, but most of the people do it because of the challenge."

Does Viemeister believe the Beale treasure exists?

"Initially I thought it was fiction," he said. "Now…"

***

Viemeister's challenge was to document the legend, not decipher the code.

The first mention of the treasure, supposedly buried in 1819 and 1821, came much later, in 1885. A 50-cent pamphlet called "The Beale Papers" was published in Lynchburg by J.B. Ward. The papers told the tale of Thomas J. Beale, who in ventures out West obtained vast quantities of gold, silver, and jewels that he brought back to Virginia in two trips.

Beale entrusted his papers, including the ciphers detailing where he secreted his treasure, to Robert Morriss, an Arlington hotelier. The published papers include correspondence between the two men before Beale disappeared without record on his third trip to the West.

Viemeister said his research has uncovered enough documentation concerning the personalities mentioned in the Beale Papers to lend them some credence. However, he conceded, that doesn't address the question of whether Ward, Beale, or someone purporting to be Beale was simply committing a brilliant hoax.

The ciphers are substitution codes. Letters in a separate document are assigned numbers, and the numbers are used to write a secret message. To decipher the message, a code breaker must first know what document to use as a key.

The Beale papers include an example using the Declaration of

Independence as key. That message provides the basic premise of the treasure being hidden in 1819 and 1821. The two other codes supposedly reveal the location of the vault and the names of Beale's associates, who were to share in the wealth.

Duran, like innumerable other Beale researchers, had searched pre-1821 publications for a document that might serve as a key.

In July 1985, Duran found a curious reference to an Adams-Owens Treaty on an old map and obtained a copy of the 1819 document from the National Archives.

By November, the numbers were working out well enough to convince him he had the key -- though it took five years to completely break the code.

Duran said the handlers of the papers had deliberately altered them as a safeguard, compounding the difficulty of the decoding.

The codes show the real story, locating the treasure "where the (old Buchanan Turnpike) road, (county) line meet fault," he said. "The River James, four bridges seen from this point."

That was enough information for Luck to move the search to the Botetourt side of the mountain, ironically just across the Blue Ridge from his farm.

The codes also radically changed the scenario of the second shipment of treasure, Duran said.

"It is my contention that the 1819 shipment was hidden in the mountain here, near Boblett's Gap. The 1821 shipment was stolen by locals."

Thomas J. Beale was really T.J. Read, Duran said. A Robert Morass (the Morriss mentioned in the papers?) and four Indians were delivering the 1821 treasure for Read when they were robbed and killed, he said, by local farmers with the names Buford, Otey, and Luck -- all ancestors of Jimmy Luck.

Duran says he has been able to document that those families came into unexplained wealth soon after 1821.

Duran also found a Bedford court document from 1820 showing that "Otey, Read and defendant called Morass" were involved in a lawsuit about collecting a judgment for a hoist. The two pieces of wood he found in the cave are what remains of the hoist, he said.

Read recovered the bodies of Morass and the Indians, which he left with a letter to Thomas Jefferson in an iron box in the cave along with the first shipment of gold, Duran said. Read then disappeared.

The codes had instructed Morass, "It's important you must get letter to Jefferson," Duran says.

Duran notes that Jefferson was familiar with the area because he had a home at Poplar Forest, southwest of Lynchburg. Jefferson was also intimately involved in the development of the West through the Louisiana Purchase and had often used ciphers for correspondence.

Duran has reams of historical documents to support his contentions. Even the presence of the Indians explains how the legend became part of Cheyenne oral history long before anything was written about the Beale treasure, he said.

"This is not derived from inspiration," Duran says of his sleuthing. "This is derived from 15 years of damn hard work."

As for the new information about his family roots, Luck shrugged his shoulders. "You can't do anything about your ancestors," he said. "That was my great, great grandfather George Luck. I didn't inherit anything out of it."

*The above article has been reprinted with permission from the Richmond Dispatch Times.

When I read the interview with Duran the memory of George Rader Brugh, Beall's best friend and keeper of the keys to the treasure code once more came back to me - - and again I've wondered; who had been responsible for Brugh's death. I recall standing and looking down on the murdered man's unmarked grave at the old Harshbarger-Munger House where I lived as a child. I didn't know then all the connections I would find.

George P. Luck, one of two sons born to John P. Luck, Botetourt County, Virginia (Black Horse Tavern), married Nannie Buford, daughter of Captain Pashal Buford in Montvale, Bedford County, Virginia. About 1822 he built "Locust Level" on the same tract of land as "Buford's Tavern," and later "Buford Airfield."

The other son, Nathan P. Luck, owned several large tracts of land, including 253 acres on either side of Harshbarger Road, Roanoke County, Virginia. He willed this land to his daughter, Fannie Dabney Luck, who married Thomas Presley Nelms in 1864. Thomas was the second son of Ebenezer (Eben) Nelms and Sinor Mitchel Nelms of Bedford County, Virginia. Thomas and Fannie built the "Nelms" house on the land her father gave her. Their youngest son, Seldon D. Nelms, (Uncle Nell) who told me his grandfather Eben and Thomas Jefferson Beall were best friends.

From that time, my life has been entangled with the story of "The Beall Treasure." My spiritual gift has led me to see people and events involved with the treasure. I'd made a vow to George Rader Brugh that when I grew up, I'd find where his family was buried and see that he was properly laid to rest with them.

As strange as it may seem, I still have that dream - and an even stronger motivation to make it a reality.

Today, with the technology of forensic science: forensic ground radar, and DNA to prove identities, I hope to have Mr. Brugh's remains located and exhumed. As of this writing, two Brugh family members have consented to provide DNA for comparison. I know this will authenticate the murdered man's identity; George Rader Brugh - and I will finally fulfill my vow.

Munger House -- This house owned by E. J. Munger at the time it was the author's home (1939-1947)

Family-- The author, Claudine Fulton Ellis with her sister Esterlene, her brother Algie, in the front yard of the Munger House at about where the "rainbow incident," would occur.

Seldon Nelms-- Uncle Nell at the old Nelms house (1947-1949)

House - The author Claudine Ellis in front of the Nelm's house (1947-1949)

Old Trail--The Old Trail the author saw in her vision of the front yard at Buford's Tavern

Padlocked Pies - The door in the Harshbarger-Munger House, where the spirit appeared to the author when she returned to look for the letter she'd placed behind the fireplace mantle (October 31, 1965)

Old Painting - Copy of the oil painting by one of the early Buford's, showing the Old Trail Road running through the yard of the home of the James Buford Family. This picture was given to the author, Claudine Ellis, by Kitty Buford Pendleton

Goose Creek Valley - Goose Creek Valley from the Blue Ridge Parkway in the 1990's

# Affidavits

**The following Affidavits were obtained
by Claudine Fulton Ellis
for the purpose of documentation for
The Beale Treasure Codes**

I, James T. Howell, owner of Buford's Tavern, also known as Locust Level, located in Montvale, VA, do hereby verify the following to be true and correct:

To my understanding, the above-mentioned Tavern was built around 1820 by Captain Pascal Buford. When I purchased the above in 1965, the original back porch of the house had been enclosed into a breezeway at the rear of the house. However, clearly visible on the original brickwork were the traces of the original construction showing that the porch had been constructed with an upper balcony. In recent years, however, I have made some structural changes in the old back porch breezeway. The addition of ceilings and walls and new doors have now concealed the view of this original construction, and it is now not visible to someone who had not previously viewed the signs of the old upper balcony on the rear porch. However, I can attest to the validity of Mrs. Ellis's description of the rear porch and the original construction of the upper balcony.

Also, one night after retiring to bed, my wife and I both heard sounds of someone approaching our bed, and suddenly we saw the ghostly figure of a man standing at our bed. The description of this event is as follows:

On this night in question, both my wife and myself had went to bed; however, neither had gone to sleep as of yet when we heard the sounds of heavy footsteps coming down the front staircase. Our bedroom was located in the west room (the old parlor room) on the first floor of the house, as the footsteps approached our bed, we both saw the figure of a man standing in our room. The ghostly figure was a tall man dressed totally in black wearing a large-brimmed hat. He approached our bed and stood at the foot of it as if staring down on the bed at us. After a couple of minutes, he turned to leave the room, and my wife said to me, "I think he wants you to follow him," however I did not. We heard his footsteps move on toward the rear of the house and seemed to go out the back door. From time to time, we have sensed his presence in the house, and we believe it to be that of Thomas Jefferson Beale (Beall). Occasionally, we have had guests or visitors here at the home who have claimed to be frightened by something that they have seen or heard that could not be explained. We just have to assume that it is Beale.

This is further documented by the story in the Roanoke Times with photos in the article "Tavern Owners see Ghost," written by Linda Grist Crewe, staff writer for the Roanoke Times, published on August 17, 1979.

I have read and agree to all references to myself as described by Mrs. Ellis, are true and correct. I do hereby give my consent and authorization to Claudine F. Ellis to use my name and all statements concerning myself and this matter within her book of the Beall Beale Treasure. I do further consent to the use of my name and all other references to myself as described by Mrs. Ellis for the purpose of the publication and sell of her book about the Beall (Beale) Treasure.

These statements are sworn before me and witnessed before me this the *29* day *of June 2000.*

_________________________________
Signed

_________________________________
Witness

_________________________________
Witness

_________________________________ My commission expires on
Notary


_________________________________

I, James T. Howell, owner of Buford's Tavern, also known as Locust Level in Montvale, Virginia, do hereby verify the following to be true and correct:

At the time of purchase of the above-mentioned property, there were several antique items that past with the Estate. Among them was an Antique Poster Bed, also there was included with the Estate a very large Antique Wicker Doll Carriage and Antique Victorian Doll. The Doll was dressed in a long white dress with a blue ribbon tied around its waist and had long blonde curls.

After the death of my wife, I sold the above doll and carriage at one of my auction sales. I do not recall who the doll and carriage was purchased by.

I have read and agree all references to myself as described by Mrs. Ellis are true and correct. I hereby do give my consent and authorization to Claudine F. Ellis to use my name, and all statements referenced to myself within her book about the Beall (Beale) Treasure. I further give my consent and authorization to Claudine F. Ellis to use my name and all other references to myself as described by Mrs. Ellis for the purpose of the publication and sell of her book about the Beall (Beale) Treasure.

These statements are hereby sworn to and witnessed before me this the _29_ day of _June 2000._

signed

witness

witness

notary

My commission expires on

JULY 25, 1996

I Barbara W Smith, of Roanoke, Va., do verify the following to be true and correct. I accompanied Claudine Fulton Ellis sometime in the early 1970's to the old home known as Buford's Tavern (or Locust Level) located in Montvale, Va. The above was located on the grounds near the remains of the once famed Buford's Tavern. However today, only a part of the chimney remains.

On our visit to the old house we learned that the present owners were now Mr and Mrs James T Howell. They had at this time also operated an antique shop on the premises. Mrs Howell graciously agreed to give Mrs Ellis and myself a tour around the property.

She showed us all of the rooms on the first and second floors of the house. In these rooms we observed some antique furnishings and other personal property that Mrs Howell told us had passed with the property when they purchased the home. Among them was a massive cannon ball bed in the east room on the second floor. In the parlor room on the first floor was an antique doll, and doll carriage. The carriage was very large and made of natural wicker. The doll had long blond curly hair and wore a long white dress, and a blue ribbon around the waist which is described by Mrs Ellis further in her story. This is the dress that had been accurately described to me by Mrs Ellis many years before the day in which I accompanied her on this visit to Locust Level, and when remembering the description I immediately recognized the doll dress as a duplicate to the dress that Mrs Ellis claims she saw herself wearing at Buford Airfield when she was a child. This is where she had had her first psychic experience that she has described in her book as being in 1938.

I have read and agree all references to myself as described by Mrs. Ellis are true and correct. I hereby do give my consent and authorization to Claudine F Ellis to use my name, and all statements referenced to myself within her book about the Beall (Beale) Treasure. I further give my consent and authorization to Claudine F.

Ellis to use my name and all other references to myself as described by Mrs Ellis for the purpose of the publication and sell of her book about the Beall (Bleale) Treasure.

These statements are hereby sworn to and witnessed before me this the *28ᵗʰ* day of *July* 1996.

_________________________________________
Signed

_________________________________________
Witness

_________________________________________
Witness

_________________________________________ My commission expires on
Notary
_________________________________________

I, Calvin B. Fulton, do verify the following information as being true and correct. I am the oldest living son of Benjamin H. Fulton and a brother to Claudine (Deanie) Fulton Ellis.

From the years of 1939 to 1947, our father rented a house owned by R.J. Munger and wife. It is further described by my sister in her book about the Beall Treasure.

I was in the Armed Forces at the time my sister Deanie found the old Bible and letter in the attic of the house; therefore, I was not present to witness it. However, over the years, she has discussed the old Bible and its contents with me numerous times.

Sometime in 1947, my parents moved from the above to a house owned by Seldon D. Nelms. My parents, with my brothers and sisters, lived there until sometime in 1949.

I give my consent and authorization to Claudine (Deanie) Fulton Ellis that the above statements may be used in the publication of her book about the Beall Treasure.

Calvin B. Fulton

Date

Given under my hand this _______ day of _______, 19___

Notary Public

My commission expires: _______, 19___

We, the undersigned, brothers and sister to Claudine F. Ellis, hereby verify the following to be true and correct.

Our family homeplace from 1939 to 1947 was the old Harshbarger House located on E. Harshbarger Road in the County of Roanoke, Virginia. It was owned at the time by E.J. Munger.

For nearly 50 years now, from time to time, our sister Claudine has discussed with us her supernatural experiences which occurred at the old house when it was our home, and how one day she was led to find a Bible in the attic; a letter signed by Thomas Jefferson Beall; envelope marked "Not to be delivered until June 1832"; and a hand-drawn map. She also believes a Mr. Brugh, sometime in the mid-1800s, died from unnatural causes in the house and was buried on the property. We believe the above story that our sister, Claudine, has shared with us over the years, which she has described in her story about the Beall treasure.

We mutually agree and give our consent and authorization to Claudine F. Ellis to use the above statements and our names in the publication of her book about the Beall treasure.

Witness

Witness

Sworn to me this ___19___ day of ___August___, 199_5_.

___________________________
Notary

My commission expires: ___Jan. 31, 1996___

I, William Eugene Brugh of Roanoke, Virginia, and I, William Ray Ball III, also of Roanoke, Virginia, mutually verify the following to be true and correct.

Sometime in the mid-1980s, we accompanied Claudine F. Ellis to the home of a Brugh family living in Salem, Virginia. We were searching for the name of George Rader Brugh. They had a genealogical chart of the Brugh family dating back to the 1700s, which listed the name George Rader Brugh. His father was an immigrant from Branchville, Germany, a valley along the Rine River. George was in the period of the time Mrs. Ellis was concerned with. We believe he was the one Mrs. Ellis had been searching for.

We mutually give our consent and authorization to Claudine F. Ellis to use the above statements and to use our names in the publication of her book about the Beale Treasure.

_______________________________  
William Eugene Brugh

_______________________________  
William Ray Ball III

Aug. 13, 1993  
Date

Aug. 13, 1993  
Date

_______________________________  
Witness

_______________________________  
Witness



Aug. 13, 1993  
Date

I, Julia E. Ball of Roanoke, Virginia, verify the following to be true and correct.

Sometime in the 1970s I accompanied Claudine F. Ellis to the home of Mr. Lainer Brugh living in the Mill Creek area of Botetourt County, Virginia.

The above had a complete genealogy record of the Brugh family which was contained in two, large loose leaf notebooks. A genealogy chart for George Rader Brugh was included. He was unmarried, had went out west and the family back east had lost contact with him. Also, Mrs. Brugh kindly allowed us to look through an old photo album of the early Brugh families. Mrs. Ellis also identified a photo which had the name George Rader Brugh written on the back side.
I give my consent and authorization to Claudine F. Ellis to use the above statements and my name in the publication of her book about the Beale treasure.

Witness

Witness

Sworn to me the _6th_ day of _July_, 199 _6_

Notary

My commission expires _May 31, 2000_

91

We, the undersigned husband and wife, Horace Hood III and Stella Hood, do hereby verify the foregoing to be true and correct.

We were, in the year 1974, members of the local Chapter of Archaeology. Sometime in the mid 1970s, we, along with several other members of the above Chapter, also from Roanoke, met with Claudine Ellis on East Hershberger Road in the City of Roanoke, Virginia. We had not previously known Mrs. Ellis. She showed us an area of land located near the end and alongside of the above road. She told us when she had lived in a nearby old house from 1939 - 1947 that the above area was part of the property. She believed a man had died in the above house from un-natural causes sometime around 1832 and was buried in an unmarked grave in the above-mentioned area. She also stated to us that she believed his last name to be Brugh. She also stated that during the time she lived in the old house, she had experienced numerous psychic phenomena, which had led her to believe this about the matter.

We mutually give our consent and authorization to Claudine (Deanie) Fulton Ellis, that the above statements may be used in the publication of her book about the "Beale" treasure.

_Horace Hood III_

Horace Hood III

_July 13, 1993_

DATE

_Stella Hood_

Stella Hood

_July 13, 1993_

DATE

_R. M. Keller_

NOTARY

My commission expires :  MY COMMISSION EXPIRES JULY 31, 1995

July 5, 1996

I, Kitty Buford Pendleton, verify that the photo-copied picture of the Buford Tavern "Locust Level" was given to Claudine Fulton Ellis by myself.

This is a valid copy of the original picture which has remained in the Buford family since the 1800s. The picture is an oil and watercolor painting which depicts the Buford Tavern along with the surrounding areas, including an old dirt trail road.

I have read and agree to all references to myself as described by Mrs. Ellis in her story, true and correct. I hereby give my consent and authorization to Claudine F. Ellis to use my name and all statements referenced to myself within her book about the Beall (Beale) Treasure. I further give my consent and authorization to Claudine F. Ellis to use my name and all other references to myself as described by Mrs. Ellis for the purpose of the publication and sell of her book about the Beall (Beale) Treasure.

These statements are hereby sworn to and witnessed before me this the _8_ day of _July_ 1996

_______________________________
signed

_______________________________
witness

_______________________________
witness

_______________________________, My commission expires on
notary

_______________________________.

I, Esterlene F. Pearce of Ford, Virginia, verify the below statements are true and correct.

I am a sister to Claudine Fulton Ellis, and I do recall having lived with my family in 1939-1947 in the old Harshbarger House, located at the above time on Harshbarger Road, in the County of Roanoke, Virginia.

During the above, I recall my sister Claudine finding in the attic a very old looking Bible, and in it was a map, a letter signed by Thomas Jefferson Beall (Beale), and an envelope addressed "Not to be delivered until June 1832." I saw the above, and Claudine kept them in the drawer of her dresser for a short time before returning them to the attic.

My sister Claudine and I have discussed for many years the above and her supernatural experiences at the above. I have heard her speak many times over the years about a buried treasure of Pots of Gold and the ill-fated death of a Mr. Brugh at the above old house.

I give my consent and authorization to Claudine F. Ellis to use the above statements, my name, and photos of myself in the publication of her book about the Beale treasure.

I give my consent and authorization to Claudine (Deanie) Fulton Ellis that the above and all references to myself may be used in the publication of her book about the Beall Treasure.

_Estherlene M. Pearce_       _10-7-'93_
                                             Date

_James T. Ellis_       _10-7-93_
Witness                                     Date

_Peggy J. Chisholm_       _Carolyn J. Spell_
Witness                                      Witness

Sworn to me the  _7th_  day of     _October_    , 199_3_

     _Mary D. Robertson_
Notary

My commission expires  _9-30-96_

I, Mildred Robinson Huffman, have read the manuscript written by Claudine (Deanie) Fulton Ellis, about the Beall Treasure.

I do verify that all the statements concerning myself and my brother George Henegar (now deceased) are true and correct.

I give my consent and authoriziation to Claudine (Deanie) Fulton Ellis that the above and all references to myself may be used in the publication of her book about the Beall Treasure.

_______________________________
Mildred Robinson Huffman

_______________________________
Date

"Given under my hand this __29__ day of __November__,
19_87_."

_______________________________
Notary Public

I, Jerry J. Hayes, of Roanoke, Virginia verify the following to be true and correct.

I have known Claudine F. Ellis for many years. Mrs. Ellis and I attended Burlington Elementary School in the 1940s, located in North County, Roanoke, Virginia. Mrs. Ellis has often talked with me over the years about a psychic experience she claims to have occurred at the old Harshbarger House when it was her home. She told me she was led to the attic of the house where she found a Bible, a map, a letter signed by Thomas Jefferson Beall, and an envelope marked "Not to be delivered until June 1832." Also, she believed a Mr. Brugh had died from unnatural causes and was buried on the property.

I have never known Mrs. Ellis to be anything other than a sincere and truthful person.

I give my consent and authorization to Claudine F. Ellis to use the above statements and my name in the publication of her book about the Beall Treasure.

Jerry J. Hayes     8-19-93
Jerry J. Hayes     Date

Witness     Witness

Sworn to me this ___19___ day of ___August___, 199_3_.

Notary

My commisison expires: ___Jan 31, 1996___

I, James T. Ellis, of Vinton, Virginia do verify the following to be true and correct.

All accounts referring to myself as described by my wife Claudine F. Ellis in her book about the Beale Treasure are accurate accounts.

I give my consent and authorization to my wife, Claudine F. Ellis to use the above statements and to use my name in the publication of her book about the Beale Treasure.

_______________________________________       Date _______________________________
James T. Ellis

_______________________________________
Witness

_______________________________________
Witness

Subscribed and sworn to before me
this _13_ day of _____, 19_93_, a Notary
Public in and for the Commonwealth of Virginia

_______________________________________

_______________________________________
Date

My Commission Expires Jan. 31, 1995

98

I, Elwood H. Journell of Roanoke, Virginia, verify the following to be true and correct.

The following is in agreement and in addition to the information contained in the affidavit my Mother, Mrs. Elua Journell Patterson, gave to Claudine F. Ellis, and which is contained in her book about the Beale Treasure.

I lived with my parents in the early 1960s at the old Harshberger House, located on East Hershberger Road in the City of Roanoke, Virginia (formerly Roanoke County).

During the above, in one of the rooms on the second floor, my Mother and I found on the right side behind a fireplace mantle, a letter headed The Declaration of Independence and was signed by Thomas Jefferson Beall (Beale). The letter was sealed in a white personal size envelope with the word "Important" written in large letters across the front.

My deceased brother, Earnest Journell, also saw the letter. He and my Mother accompanied me to Hollins College in Roanoke County, Virginia. We discussed the unknown importance of the letter with a history professor, Dr. Carl Ramsey. He informed us that he had a friend in which he intended to seek consultation, with the hopes they could together learn of the letter's importance.

We left the letter in Dr. Ramsey's care, and this was sometime in the early 1960s. To date, I do not know of the letter's whereabouts or if it even still exists.

However, since the above time, I learned from Claudine F. Ellis the intended use and importance of the above letter. It is as follows:

My Mother and I first met Mrs. Ellis one Sunday morning, sometime around 1967 when we resided on Dale Avenue, S.E., in the City of Roanoke. At this time Mrs. Ellis informed us that she had lived with her parents from 1939-1947 at the old Harshberger House located on East Hershberger Road. This was the same property my father had purchased in the 1960s, and for a time, had also been our home place. Mrs. Ellis told us during the time of the above when the old house had been her home, she found in the attic a very old looking Bible. Contained in the Bible was a letter headed the Declaration of Independence dated May 15, and was signed by Thomas Jefferson Beall (Beale); an envelope (not to be delivered until June 1832) and also a map. She told us she made a copy of the letter, sealed it in a white personal size envelope and hid it on the right side behind a fireplace mantle in one of the rooms on the second floor.

Mrs. Ellis was so precise in her description of the letter and its place of concealment that my Mother and I both knew beyond any doubt that Mrs. Ellis had to have been the person to have put the letter behind the fireplace mantle.

I give my consent and authorization to Claudine F. Ellis to use the above statements and my name in the publication of her book about the Beale treasure.


_Elwood A. Burnell_        _Oct 25 1993_
                                        Date

_Kathleen H. Clark_        _10-25-9-93_
    (Witness)                                Date

_Lillian F. Wilson_
Witness                                              Witness

Sworn to me the _25TH_ day of _OCTOBER_, 199_3_

_[Notary signature]_
Notary

My commission expires _AUGUST 31, 1997_

I, W.R. Palmer and wife Edna Palmer of Roanoke, Virginia verify the following to be true and correct.

We both were witnesses and took part in the documentary video done on December 2, 1989 at the Liberty House retirement home in Roanoke, Virginia were Enda's mother, Mrs. Eula Journell Patterson was a resident. Claudine F. Ellis and William E. Brugh were also present and took part in the above documentary along with Mrs. Eula Journell Patterson. Two employees of the above home were also present as witnesses.

We further verify that Mrs. Patterson stated to us many times over she had found a letter with the word "Important" written on the envelope behind a fireplace mantle in one of the rooms on the second floor when she lived in the old Harshbarger house on E. Harshbarger Road in the City of Roanoke. At this time she and her husband, Mr. Journell, bought the property around 1960. Also, we recall hearing Mrs. Patterson's two son's discuss the same above letter.

We mutually give our consent and authorization to Claudine F. Ellis, to use the above video including any statements, and both our names in the publication of her book about the Beale treasure.

_______________________________        _______________________________
W.R. Palmer                             Edna Palmer

_______________________________        _______________________________
Date                                    Date

_______________________________        _______________________________
Witness                                 Witness

Given under my hand this _______ day of _______________, 19___

_______________________________
Date

My commission expires: _______________________________

June 15, 1996

To whom it may concern:
I _Alice Cassell Tuckwiller,_ Librarian for the Roanoke City Public
Library verify the following to be true and correct.

That we have on micro-fiche in the Virginia Room the following
articles published in the Roanoke Times and World News on Sunday,
August 17, 1975.

Article One: Roanoke Times "Tempo," Features Family Gardens
Section E. (A Ghost Story) Rocky Mount VA. "Thump---Thump--
Thump, There's Nobody There," by Times Staff Writer Linda Grist
Crewe. Times Photo by John Cook, (Amos House, Rocky Mount
VA).

Article Two: Featured on lower half of above mentioned page, "A
Beale Ghost Story," as told by Mrs. James Howell, Owner of Buford's
Tavern, Montvale VA. Times Photos by Betty Masters, included
"Haunted Stairs" and "Mrs. James Howell, Straightens Ghost's Bed."

Copies were made of these articles by myself for Mrs. Claudine
Fulton Ellis on _June 15, 1996_.

These statements were sworn before me on this Day _15th_ of _June_
1996. Signed _Dawn Hale._
Notary. My commission expires on _May 31, 2000_.

# GENEALOGY OF THE BEALL FAMILIES

Alexander Beall I, the Immigrant-Continued

Mary Beall, b 1694; m Lingan Wilson.
In her father Alexander's will of 1743 he leaves to "Lingan Wilson's wife Mary a chaise and harnais."
Lingan Wilson testator in the will of Thomas Lingan, made Aug. 20, 1722, Calvert County. Liber 20, folio 213.

Lingan Wilson was a member of Captain Samuel Magruder's Company of P. G. Co. Militia of 1748. Md. Hist. Mag., Vol. VI, folio 48.

The will of Mrs. Elizabeth Hepburn, dated Feb. 4, 1734, Liber 21, folio 266, P. G. Co., 1734, widow of Dr. Patrick Hepburn. She seems to have m 5 times.

m [1] a Beall and had a dr, Elizabeth Beall

m [2] George Scott. Issue: 1, Elizabeth Scott, with a daughter, Elizabeth Scott; 2, a daughter who m John Hepburn.

m [3]- Wilson. Had a son, Lingan Wilson, who had two children, Lingan and Mary.

m [4]- Dick. Had a son whom Margaret.

m [5] Dr. Patrick Hepburn. Issue unknown. Mrs. Patrick Hepburn mentions in her will two grandchildren named Mary and
Lingan Wilson.

One authority says Alexander Beall m Elizabeth, whose mother was named Elizabeth, a widow, who m Dr. Patrick Hepburn. She'd 1735.

F. 'William Beall of Alexandria, b 1700, d 1769. m Sarah Magruder, b 1713, dr of Ninian Magruder, Sr., and his wife, Elizabeth Brewer.

A deposition made 1734 before a Court in P. G. Co., Book T, folio 209, William Beall stated his age was 34 years.

In his father's will of 1743 he gets land called Largoe, and Newfoundland, bath lyeth on the south side of southwest branch of the Patuxent River. William Beall transferred land to Christopher Lowndes, July 20, 1738. LiberT, folio 633, P. G. Co.

Lowndes built a large brick house on this land near Bladenshurg. It is in excellent condition today (1914). He called it Bostock. Wash, Star, April 12, 1914.

William and Sarah had issue:

1. William Beall of William, b 1733. Mentioned for pay as a private for service in French and Indian War, 1757-8. Md. Hist. Mag., Vol. V of 1914, folio 349.

Signed a petition in 1758, to divide All Souls' Parish in Frederick County. Scharf's Hist. W. Md., folios 503, 745.

Member Association of Freemen, 1775, at Frederick City, 1,561

members. Md. Hist. Mag., Vol. XI of 1916, folio 163.

Jan. 30, Md. Arch., 1776, in Rawlins Regiment, Continental Line of Md. Md. Arch. VOl. XVIII, folio 9.

Feb. 8, 1779, enlisted in Rawlins' Regiment, Continental Line of Md. Md. Arch., Vol. XVIII folio 90.

2. Sarah Beall, b 1735, d 1805.

m Zachariah Magruder, son of Samuel Magruder, Sr. Issue:

[1] William Beall Magruder.

[2] Eleanor Magruder.

[3] Samuel Beall Magruder.

[4] Richard Magruder.

[5] Josiah Magruder.

[6] Norman Bruce Magruder. In pension report of 1835 as enlisting from Maryland.

[7] Nathaniel Magruder.

[8] Elizabeth Magruder.

3. Ninian Magruder Beall, b 1737, d 1759.

m Eleanor Magruder b 1732, dr of John Magruder, son of Ninian. Will probated 1759. LiberA I, folio 119, Frederick Co.

In French and Indian War of 1757-8, Md. Hist. Mag., Vol. IX of 1914, folio 361. He returned from the war in a feeble condition,

In his will he mentions his wife Eleanor, an expected posthumous child, and the following brothers and sisters, viz.: Ruth Ogle, Mordecai, Zepheniah, Zecheriah, Phillip, William, Elizabeth, James and Sarah.

4. Mordecai Beall, b 1742, d 1777; m Elizabeth Beall b 1743,

dr of Nathania! Beall, d 1757.

Mustered for pay as clerk in Captain Joshua Beall's Company in French and Indian War, 1757-8. Md. Hist. Mag., Vol. IX of 1914, folio 355.

Commissioned First Lieutenant by the Committee of Observation, in Captain Robert Wood's Company, Frederick Co. Militia, Nov.29, 1775. Md. Hist. Mag., Vol. XI of 1915, folios 53 and 316.
In 1775 member Association of Freemen at Frederick City, 1561 members. Md. Hist. Mag., Vol. XI of 1915, folio 163. Captain in Frederick Co. Militia, 37th Battalion, May 11,
1776
Md. arch., Vol. XI, folio 427.

## Mordecai and Elizabeth had issue:
1. Nathaniel Beall, b 1758; m Hannah. The land records of Berkeley County, W.Va., indicate that Nathaniel Beall and his wife Hannah went from Maryland to Frederick County, Va., then to Berkeley County, W. Va., and in 1789 were located in Washington County, Pa.

[2] Colmore Beall, b 1760, d 1840. Moved from Maryland to Washington Co., Pa., then before 1818 went to Harrison Co., Ohio.

m . ______Issue:

a. John Beall, b 1780.

b. Alexander Beall, b 1782 in Pa. Went to Harrison Co., Ohio, before 1823.

m . ______Issue:

[a], Coleman; [b], Edmund Thomas, b 1819 in Pa., brought to Harrison Co., Ohio, in 1823, then went to Keene, Coshocton Co., Ohio, then to Adams Co., Ind.; [c], Liverton; [d], Robert; [e],
Parker; [f ], Rhoda, m ______ Snyder; [g], Sarah, m Means; [h], Hiram, m Wood; [i], Alexander.

c .James Beall, b 1784.

d. Hileary Beall, b 1786.

e. Daniel Beall, b 1788.

f.Colemore Beall, b 1790.

***g.Thomas Beall, b 1792.**

h. Mary Ann Beall, b 1794; m Aaron Yarmell.

i. Elizabeth Beall, b 1796; m ______ McCoy.

k. Rebecca Beall, b 1798; m ______ Smith.

l. Casandra Beall, b 1800; m Taylor.

m. Sarah Beall, b 1802; m April 24, 1834, John Smith of Harrison Co., Ohio.

n. Nancy Beall, b 1804.

o. Margaret Beall, b 1806.

p. Eliza Beall, b 1808.

q. Jane Beall, b 1810.

r. Minerva Beall, b 1812.

[3] William Beall, b 1762.

[4] Nancy Beall, b 1764.

[5] Sarah Beall, b 1766.

[6] Elijah Beall, b 1768.

[7] Mordecai Beall, b 1770.

[8] Martha Beall, b 1772.

[9] Elizabeth Beall, b 1774.

See grandmother Orme's estate settlement, Liber B V, No. 1, folio 162, Frederick Co., 1807.

5. Ruth Beall, b 1741; m ______Ogle.

6. Zachariah Beall, b 1743; m Rebecca Tyson. Located in NW

100 of Frederick Co., in the Census of 1776. Moved to North Carolina in 1778. Issue:

[1] Horatio Beall, b 1774; m Elizabeth Harris.

[2] Jennie Beall, b 1776; m Joseph Albra.

[3] Jemima Beall, b 1780; m John FitzGerald.

[4] Drucilla Beall, b 1785; m John Gaither.

[5] Dr. Asa Beall, b 1790. In N. C. Census of 1790. Moved to Georgia and m Susan Remsen of Ga. Issue:

a. Benjamin L. Beall, b 1827 in Lincoln Co., Ga; m [1] Mary P. Hawkins; m [2] Jane E. Alexander.

b. Harriet Beall, b 1829; m Dr. M. H. Tuff, of Augusta.

[6] Rebecca Beall, b 1797; m Sandy Kilpatrick.

[7] Dr. Burgess Lamar Beall, b 1799 in Ivedell Co., N. C.
7. Elizabeth Beall, b 1745.
8. Phillip Beall, b 1747.
9. James Magruder Beall, b 1749, d 1834 in Berkeley Co., W. Va.
Member Association of Freemen, Frederick Co., Dec. 27, 1775, 1,561 members. Md. Hist. Mag., Vol. XI of 1916, folio 163. Nov. 29, 1775, sergeant in Captain Robert Woods' Company, Frederick Co. Militia. Md. Hist. Mag., Vol. X of 1915, folio 53. in Margaret and went to Berkeley Co., XV. Va. Issue:
[1] Zebulon Beall, b 1770; m Rachel.
[2] James Beall, b 1772. Settled in Champaign Co., Ohio. Went to Sagamore Co., Ill.
[3] William Beall, b 1774; m Rosanria. Settled in Champaign Co., Ohio.
[4] Adam Beall, b 1776; m 1834; was in Berkeley Co., W.Va.
10. Zepheniah Beall, b Feb. 15, 1753, d June 15, 1809. June 25, 1776, Ensign in Captain Orme's Company, 16<sup>th</sup> Battalion, Frederick Co. Militia. Md. Arch., Vol. XI, folio 357.
Sept. 12, 1777, 2nd Lieut. Lower Battalion, Montgomery Co. Militia. Md. Arch., Vol. XVI, folio 373.
Sept. 12, 1779, Ensign Middle Battalion, Montgomery Co. Militia. Md. Arch., Vol. XI, folio 357.
Took patriots' oath in Montgomery Co., 1778.
mAnn Beall, b 1756, d 1820.
Went to Berkeley Co., W.Va., in 1791 and prospered.
Zepheniah Beall recorded April 4, 1806, at Martinsburg, W.Va., about bill of sale of Negroes to Francis Silver. Issue:
(1) Ann Beall, b 1789; m 1802 Francis Silver, b 1775, d 1852. Issue:
a. Zepheniah Silver, b 1803; m Martha Jane Henshaw. Part issue 2 sons;
(a) Francis Silver, b ______; m Mary Ann Gray, and had son, Gray Silver. See page 308, Minute Man, October, 1927, S.A.R.
(b) John Moore Silver b ______; m Margaret Davis Perkins. Had son, Bayard Perkins Silver, of St. Louis, Mo. See page 389, Minute Man for October, 1927, S.A.R.

b. Jeremiah Silver, b 1805.

c. Anne Silver, b 1807

d. Lucy Semple Silver, b 1809

    (2) Lucy Beall, b 1790; m James Waggener.

    (3) Mary Beall, b 1791; m (1) Samuel Blackmore; m (2) Jacob Jobe.

    (4) Eleanor Beall, b 1795, d 1867; m Samuel Silver.

Above records of Christ Episcopal Church of Berkeley Co., W.Va.

*It is the author's belief that this Thomas Beall is the Beall of the "Beall Treasure." This contention is based on information provided by Uncle Nelms: Thomas Jefferson Beall had five brothers, and he was the youngest. This is the only Thomas Beall with five older brothers.

# Muster Roll of Boat Synia (13)

Major Daniel Holliday, Captain & one (of) the Com.
for internal regulation of Miss. Territory
William Richardson- Captain & Treasurer of Boston
Stephen Donohoc-one of Com, for internal reg & has
charge of the spirits, Alexandria, Virg.
Walter Nash Do Do.-& one of the managers in the
cooking depart., Miss Terr.
Henry Burt Esq. Trader, From N. York
Maj. Nelson, assistant to cooking department -
Pennsylvania

*** Capt. Thos. J. Beall common passenger
from Harpers Ferry**
Henry Wilkins Do Do -Pittsburg
Mount Do -Alexandria, Virginia
Doct L.S. Parmeley Do Do- Boston, Mass.
Mr. McAdams- Steersman
Morris- Oarsma
Stone- Do
Bill- Do
Lewis- Do
Limerick- Cook- Black- belonging to Maj
Halliday
Daniel Boy-Do - belonging to Nash

---

17 Persons

---

The following is a list of letters left at the post office in Franklin, Missouri in 1820 including mail for *Beall, **Buford, ***Hart and ****Morris. This list has been reproduced from the original.

## *LIST OF LETTERS*

**R**EMAINING in the Post Office at
FRANKLIN, Missouri, on the 31". day
of March, 1820, which if not taken out
within three months will be sent to the
General Post Office as dead letters.

### *A*

Allen Isaac

Allyn Isaac

Alley William

Allen Spenser

Arnold Price

Allison Ephraim

Armstrong Solomon


Alcut James

Armstrong Jacob

Ashlock Josiah

Avreth Won or John
Cornelius

Anderson James

Anderson Caleb G

Alock Elijah

Adams Abram

Asher Samuel

### *B*

Bell John

Bartlett Wm S

Berry Taylor Maj.

Belmear Samuel

Brock Joshua

Barton Joshua

Baber Hiriam H

Barns James

Bradley Thomas

Blevens David

Barnett William

Bower William
James

Brown John

Blackwell John F

***Beall Thomas**

Beters Sally

Boyse George T

Bradley Sion

Barnes Richard

Barns Thomas

Bradly Joseph

Boyce Willis

Bamett Addam S

Bracken Charles

Brown Mildred

Boone Daniel col or
Jesse or Nathan
Boone
Barnes Frederick
Bleven John Dr
Belcher Isam
Barbee William
Bass Peter
**Buford William**
Burroughs George
Beschour John
Brackon John C

Bullard Reuben
Brashear Walter Dr
Bird James
Bell George
Boone Morgan
Boles Flam
Baroon Sarah
Brown Rose mrs
Briscoe Truman
Barbee William
Boone William col
Blakeslee William

## H

Houston William L
Holt Jacob H
Harden William
Hix John
Holeman Joseph or
William
Hughes Green
***Hart Miles**

Hanks William
Huston Sally
Hubbard Samuel
Howard Hammel
Hutchinson John
Hargis Isaac D
Hull Henry J

## M

Murphy William
Miller Samuel
M'Mibin Alexander
M'Bride Thomas
Morris Nathaniel
Murrill Isaac
M'Gee James
M'Pheters Addam

Mitchell Richard
Monnicle Christopher
Monroe William
Mathery Nancy
M'Clanahan Abraham
Miller Sebum J
M'Daniel Joshua
****Morris Robert W**

**The following pages are
numbered according to
the original Beale Papers**

# "The Beale Papers"

"The following details of an incident that happened many years ago, but which has lost none of its interest on that account, are now given to the public for the first time.

"Until now, for reasons which will be apparent to every one, all knowledge of this affair was confined to a very limited circle--to the writer's immediate family, and to one old and valued friend, upon whose discretion he could always rely. Nor was it ever intended to travel beyond that circle. But circumstances over which he had no control, pecuniary embarrassments of a pressing character, and duty to a dependent family requiring his undivided attention, force him to abandon a task to which he has devoted the best years of his life, but which seems as far from accomplishment as at the start. He is, therefore, compelled, however unwillingly, to relinquish to others the elucidation of the Beale Papers, not doubting that of the many who will give the subject attention, some one, through fortune or accident, will speedily solve their mystery and secure the prize which has eluded him.

It can be readily imagined that this course was not determined upon all at once. Regardless of the entreaties of his family and the persistent advice of his friends, who were formerly as sanguine as himself, he stubbornly continued his investigations, until absolute want stared him in the face and forced him to yield to their persuasions. Having now lost all hope of benefit from this source to himself, he is not unwilling that others may receive it, and only hopes that the prize may fall to some poor, but honest man, who will use his discovery not solely for the promotion of his own enjoyment, but for the welfare of others.

Until the writer lost all hope of ultimate success, he toiled faithfully at his work. Unlike any other pursuit with practical and natural results, a charm attended it, independent of the ultimate benefit he expected; and the possibility of success lent an interest and excitement to the work not to be resisted.

It would be difficult to portray the delight he experienced when accident revealed to him the explanation of paper 'No. 2'.

Unmeaning, as this had hitherto been, it was now fully explained, and no difficulty was apprehended in mastering the others. But this accident, affording so much pleasure at the time, was a most unfortunate one for him, as it induced him to neglect family, friends, and all legitimate pursuits for what has proved, so far, the veriest illusion.

It will be seen by a perusal of Mr. Beale's letter to Mr. Morriss that he promised, under certain contingencies, such as failure to see or communicate with him in a given time, to furnish a key by which the papers would be fully explained.

As the failure to do either actually occurred, and the promised explanation has never been received, it may possibly remain in the hands of some relative or friend of Beale's, or some other person engaged in the enterprise with him. That they would attach no importance to a seemingly unintelligible writing seems quite natural; but their attention being called to them by the publication of this narrative, may result in eventually bringing to light the missing papers.

Mr. Beale, who deposited with Mr. Morriss the papers which form the subject of this history, is described as being a gentleman well educated, evidently of good family, and with popular manners. What motives could have influenced him and so many others to risk their health and their lives in such an undertaking, except the natural love of daring adventure, with its consequent excitement, we can only conjecture.

We may suppose, and indeed we have his word for so doing, that they were infatuated with the dangers, and with the wild and roving character of their lives, the charms of which lured them farther and farther from civilization, until their lives were sacrificed to their temerity. This was the opinion of Mr. Morriss, and in this way only can we account for the fact that the treasure for which they sacrificed so much, constituting almost fabulous wealth, lies abandoned and unclaimed for more than half a century.

Should any of my readers be more fortunate than myself in discovering its place of concealment, I shall not only rejoice with them, but feel that I have at least accomplished something in contributing to the happiness of others.

## THE LATE ROBERT MORRIS

"Robert Morriss, the custodian of the Beale Papers, was born in 1778 in the State of Maryland, but removed at an early age with his family to Loudoun County, Virginia, where, in 1803, he married Miss Sarah Mitchell, a fine looking and accomplished young lady of that county.

"In obtaining such a wife, Mr. Morriss was peculiarly fortunate, as her subsequent career fully demonstrated. As a wife she was without reproach, as a generous and sympathizing woman she was without an equal--the poor will long remember her charities, and lament the friend they have lost.

"Shortly after his removal to Lynchburg, Mr. Morriss engaged in the mercantile business, and shortly thereafter, he became a purchaser and shipper of tobacco to an extent hitherto unknown in this section. In this pursuit he was eminently successful for several years, and speedily accumulated a comfortable independence.

"It was during this period of his success that Mr. Morriss erected the first brick building of which the town could boast, and which still stands on Main Street, a monument to his enterprise. His private residence, the house now owned and occupied by Max Gugenheimer, Esquire, at the head of Main Street, I think he also built. There the most unbounded hospitality reigned, and every facility for enjoyment was furnished. The elite of the town assembled there more frequently than elsewhere, and there are now living some whose pleasant recollections are associated with that period.

"The happiness of Mr. Morriss, however, was of short duration, for reverses came when they were least expected. Heavy purchases of tobacco, at ruinous figures, in anticipation of an upward market, which visions were never realized, swept from him in a moment the savings of years, and left him nothing save his honor and the sincere sympathy of the community, with which to begin the battle anew.

"It was at this time that Mrs. Morriss exhibited the loveliest traits of her character. Seeminly unmindful of her condition, with a smiling fact and cheering words, she so encouraged her husband that he became almost reconciled to his fate.

"Thrown thus upon his own resources, by the advice of his wife, Mr. Morriss leased for a term of years the Washington Hotel, known now as the Arlington, on Church Street, and commenced the business of hotel keeping. His kind disposition, strict probity, excellent management, and well-ordered household, soon rendered him famous as a host, and his reputation extended even to other States. His was the house par excellence of the town, and no fashionable assemblages met at any other.

"Finding, in a few years, that his experiment was successful and his business remunerative, he removed to the Franklin Hotel, now the Norvell House, the largest and best arranged in the city. This house he conducted for many years, enjoying the friendship and countenance of the first men of the country. Amongst his guests and devoted friends were Jackson, Clay, Coles, Witcher, Chief Justice Marshall and a host of others scarcely less distinguished might be enumerated.

"But it was not the wealth and distinguished alone who appreciated Mr. Morriss. The poor and lowly had blessings for the man who sympathized with their misfortunes and was ever ready to relieve their distress. Many poor but worthy families, whose descendants are now in our midst, can remember the fact that his table supplied their daily food, not for days and weeks only, but for months at a time. And, as a further instance of his forebearance and unparalleled generosity, there are now living those who will testify to the fact that he permitted a boarder, in no way connected with him, to remain in his house for more than twenty years, and until he died, without ever receiving the slightest remuneration, and that he was never made to feel otherwise than as a favored guest.

"In manner Mr. Morriss was courteous and gentle; but when occasion demanded, he could be stern and determined, too. He was emphatically the master of his house, and from his decision there was no appeal. As an "old Virginia gentleman", he was <u>sans peur et sans reproche</u>, and to a remarkable extent possessed the confidence and affection of his friends.

"After a checquered and eventful life of more than eighty years, passed mostly in business, which brought him in contact with all classes of people, he died, lamented by all,' leaving not an enemy behind. His death, which occurred in 1863, was just two years subsequent to that of his wife. It can be truly said that no persons ever lived in a community for such a length of time who accomplished more good during their lives, of whose death was more universally regretted.

"It was the unblemished character of the man, and the universal confidence reposed in him, that induced Beale to entrust him with his secret, and, in certain contingencies, select him for a most important post. That his confidence was not misplaced every one remembering Mr. Morriss will acknowledge.

"It was in 1862, the second year of the Confederate war, that Mr. Morriss first intimated the possession of a secret that was destined to make some persons wealthy. At first, he was not very communicative, nor did I press him to reveal what he seemed to speak of with reluctance. In a few weeks, however, his mind seemed changed, and he voluntarily proffered his confidence.

"Inviting me to his room, with no one to interrupt us, he gave me an outline of the matter, which soon enlisted my interest and created an intense longing to learn more. About this time, however, affairs of importance required my presence in Richmond, and prevented further communication between us until after my return when I found Mr. Morriss ready to resume the interesting subject. A private interview was soon arranged and, after several preliminaries had been complied with, the papers upon which this history is based were delivered into my possession.

"The reasons which influenced Mr. Morriss in selecting me for the trust he gave were, in substance, as follows: First, friendship for myself and family, whom he would benefit it he could. Second, the knowledge that I was young and in circumstances to afford leisure for the task imposed. And, finally, a confidence that I would regard his instructions and carry out his wishes regarding his charge. These, and perhaps others, he gave during our frequent conversations upon the subject; and doubtless, he believed he was conferring a favor which would redound greatly to my advantage. That it has proved otherwise is a misfortune to me, but no fault of his.

"The conditions alluded to above were that I should devote as much time as was practicable to the papers he had given me; master, if possible, their contents, and if successful in deciphering their meaning and eventually finding the treasure, to appropriate one-half of his portion as a remuneration for my services, the other half to be distributed to certain relatives and connections of his own, whose names he gave me; the remainder to be held by me in trust for the benefit of such claimants as might at any time appear and be able to authenticate their claims. This latter amount to be left intact subject to such demands for the space of twenty years, when, if still unclaimed, it should revert to myself or my heirs, as a legacy from himself.

"As there was nothing objectionable in this, the required promise was given, and the box and contents were placed in my possession.

"When the writer recalls his anxious hours, his midnight vigils, his toil, his hopes and disappointments, all consequent upon this promise, he can only conclude that the legacy of Mr. Morriss was not as he designed it--a blessing in disguise.

"Having assumed the responsibilities and consented to the requirements of Mr. Morriss, I determined to devote as much time to the accomplishment of the task as could be consistently spared from other duties. With this purpose in view, I requested from Mr. Morriss a statement of every particular connected with the affair or having the slightest bearing upon it, together with such views and opinions of his own as might ultimately benefit me in my researches. In reply, he gave me the following, which I reduced to writing and filed with the papers for future reference:

"It was in the month of January 1820, while keeping the Washington Hotel, that I first saw and became acquainted with Beale. In company with two others, he came to my house seeking entertainment for himself and friends. Being assured of a comfortable provision for themselves and their horses, Beale stated his intention of remaining for the winter, should nothing occur to alter his plans, but that the gentlemen accompanying him would leave in a few days for Richmond, near which place they resided; and that they were anxious to reach their homes, from which they had long been absent.

"They all appeared to be gentlemen, and with a free and independent air, which rendered them peculiarly attractive. After remaining a week or ten days, the two left, with expressions of satisfaction with their visit. Beale, who remained, soon became a favored and popular guest. His social disposition and friendly demeanor rendered him extremely popular with everyone, particularly the ladies, and a pleasant and friendly intercourse was quickly established between them.

"In person Beale was about six feet in height, with jet black eyes, and hair of the same color, worn longer than was the style at that time. His form was symmetrical and gave evidence of unusual strength and activity. But his distinguishing feature was a dark and swarthy complexion, as if much exposure to the sun and weather had thoroughly tanned and discolored him.

"This, however, did not detract from his appearance; and I thought him the handsomest man I had ever seen. Altogether, he was a model of manly beauty, favored by the ladies and envied by the men. To the first, he was reverentially tender and polite; to the latter, affable and courteous when they kept within bounds, but if they were supercilious or presuming, the lion was aroused, and woe to the man who offended him. Instances of that character occurred more than once while he was my guest, and always resulted in his demanding and receiving an apology. His character soon became universally known, and he was no longer troubled by impertinence.

"Such a man was Thomas Jefferson Beale, as he appeared in 1820, and in his subsequent visits to my house. He registered simply from Virginia, but I am of the impression he was from some western portion of the state. Curiously enough, he never adverted to his family or to his antecedents, nor did I question him concerning them, as I would have done had I dreamed of the interest that in the future would attach to his name.

"Mr. Beale remained with me until about the latter end of the following March, when he left with the same friends who first accompanied him to my house and who had returned some days before.

"After this I heard nothing from Mr. Beale until January, 1822, when he once more made his appearance, the same genial and popular gentleman as before, but if possible, darker and swarthier than ever. His welcome was a genuine one as all were delighted to see him.

"In the spring at about the same time, he again left. But before doing so, Beale handed to me this box, which, as he said, contained papers of value and importance, and which he desired to leave in my charge until called for hereafter. Of course, I did not decline to receive them, but little imagined their importance until his letter from St. Louis was received. This letter I carefully preserved, and it will be given with these papers.

"The box was of iron, carefully locked and of such weight as to render it a safe depository for articles of value. I placed it in a safe and secure place, where it could not be disturbed until such time as it should be demanded by its owner.

"The letter I alluded to above was the last communication I ever received from Beale, and I never saw him again. I can only suppose that he was killed by Indians, afar from his home, though nothing more was heard of his death. His companions, too, must all have shared his fate as no one has ever demanded the box or claimed his effects.

"The box was left in my hands in the spring of 1822 and, by authority of his letter, I should have examined its contents in 1832, ten years thereafter, having heard nothing from Beale in the meantime. But it was not until 1845, some 23 years after it came into my possession, that I decided upon opening it. During that year, I had the lock broken, and, with the exception of the two letters to myself, and some old receipts, found only some unintelligible papers, covered with figures, and totally incomprehensible to me.

"According to his letter, these papers convey all the information necessary to find the treasure he has concealed, and upon you devolves the responsibility of recovering it. Should you succeed you will be amply reimbursed for your work, and others near and dear to me will likewise be benefitted. The end is worth all your exertions, and I have every hope that success will reward your efforts.

"Such, in substance, was the statement of Mr. Morriss in answer to the various interrogatories propounded to him. And finding that I could elicit no further information, I resolved to do the best I could with the limited means at my disposal.

"I commenced by reading over and over again the letters to Mr. Morriss, endeavoring to impress each syllable they contained on my memory, and to extract from them, if possible, some meaning or allusion that might give a faint or barely perceptible hint as a guide. No such clue, however, could I find, and where or how to commence was a problem I found most difficult to solve.

"To systematize a plan for my work, I arranged the papers in the order of their length, and numbered them, designing to commence with the first and devote my whole attention to that until I had either unraveled its meaning or was convinced of its impossibility--afterwards to take up the others, and proceed as before.

"All of this I did in the course of time, but failed so completely that my hopes of solving the mystery were well nigh abandoned. My thoughts, however, were constantly upon it, and the figures contained in each paper, in their regular order, were fixed in my memory. My impression was that each figure represented a letter, but as the numbers so greatly exceeded the letters of the alphabet, I wondered if it were possible that some document had been used, and the words numbered.

"With this idea in mind, a test was made of every book I could produce by numbering the letters and comparing their numbers with those of the manuscript. All to no purpose, however, until the Declaration of Independence afforded the clew to one of the papers, and revived my hopes.

"To enable my readers to better understand the explanation of this paper, the Declaration of Independence is given herewith, the words numbered in consecutive order. I am sure this will be of interest to those designing to follow up my investigations.

"When I first made this discovery, I thought I had the key to the whole, but soon ascertained that further work was necessary before my task could be completed. The encouragement afforded however by this discovery, enabled me to proceed and I have persisted in my labors to the present time. Now, as I have already said, I am forced by circumstances to devote my time to other pursuits and to abandon hopes which were destined never to be realized.

"The following is the letter addressed to Mr. Morriss by Beale and dated St. Louis, May, 1822, and was the latest communication ever received from him."

St. Louis, Mo., May 9, 1822

Robt. Morriss, Esq.
My esteemed friend:

Ever since leaving my comfortable quarters at your house I have been journeying to this place, and only succeeded in reaching it yesterday. I had had, altogether, a pleasant time, the weather being fine and the atmosphere bracing. I shall remain here a week or ten days longer, then "ho" for the plains, to hunt buffalo and encounter the savage grizzlies. How long I may be absent I cannot now determine, certainly not less than two years, perhaps longer.

With regard to the box left in your charge I have a few words to say and, if you will permit me, give you some instructions concerning it. It contains papers vitally affecting the fortunes of myself and many others engaged in business with me, and in the event of my death its loss might be irreparable. You will, therefore, see the necessity of guarding it with vigilance and care to prevent so great a catastrophe. It also contains some letters addressed to yourself and which will be necessary to enlighten you concerning the business in which we are engaged. Should none of us ever return, you will please preserve carefully the box for a period of ten years from the date of this letter, and if I, or no one with authority from me, during that time demands its restoration, you will open it, which can be done by removing the lock.

You will find, in addition to the papers addressed to you, other papers which will be unintelligible without the aid of a key to assist you. Such a key I have left in the hands of a friend in this place, sealed, addressed to yourself, and endorsed "Not to be delivered until June,

122

1832." By means of this you will understand fully all you will be required to do.

I know you will cheerfully comply with this request, thus adding to the many obligations under which you have already placed me. In the meantime, should death or sickness happen to you, to which all are liable, please select from among your friends some one worthy, and to him hand this letter, and to him delegate your authority.

I have been thus particular in my instructions in consequence of the somewhat perilous enterprise in which we are engaged, but trust we shall meet long ere the time expires, and so save you this trouble. Be the result what it may, however, the game is worth the candle and we will play it to the end.

With kindest wishes for your most excellent wife, compliments to the ladies, a good word to enquiring friends, if there be any, and assurances of my highest esteem for yourself, I remain, as ever,

Your sincere friend,
Tho$^S$ . Jeff$^n$ . Beale.


"After the reception of this letter, Mr. Morriss states that he was particularly careful to see the box securely placed, where it could remain in absolute safety so long as the exigencies of the case might require. The letter, too, he was equally careful to preserve for future use should it be needed.

"Having done all that was required of him, Mr. Morriss could only await Beale's return, or some communication from him. In either case, he was disappointed, nor did a line or message ever reach him.

"During this period, rumors of Indian outrages and massacres were current, but no mention of Beale's name ever occurred. What became of him and his companions is left entirely to conjecture. Whether he was slain by Indians, or killed by the savage animals of the Rocky Mountains, or whether exposure, and perhaps privation, did its work can never be told. One thing at least is certain, that of the young and gallant band, whose buoyant spirits led them to seek such a life and to forsake the comforts of home, with all its enjoyments, for the dangers and privations they must necessarily encounter, not a survivor remains.

"Though Mr. Morriss was aware of the contents of the box in 1845, it was not until 1862, forty years after he received it, that he thought proper to mention its existence, and to myself alone did he then divulge it. He had become long since satisfied that the parties were no longer living, but his delicacy of feeling prevented him assuming as a fact a matter so pregnant with consequences. He frequently decided upon doing so, and as often delayed it for another time. And when, at last, he did speak of the matter, it was with seeming reluctance, as if he felt he was committing a wrong. But the story once told, he evinced up to the time of his death the greatest interest in my success, and in frequent interviews encouraged me to proceed.

"It is now more than twenty years since these papers came into my hands, and, with the exception of one of them, they are still as incomprehensible as ever. Much time was devoted to this one, and those who engage in the matter will be saved what has been consumed upon it myself.

"Before giving the papers to the public, I would say a word to those who may take an interest in them, and give them a little advice, acquired by bitter experience. It is to devote only such time as can be spared from your legitimate business to the task, and, if you can spare no time, let the matter alone. Should you disregard my advice, do not hold me responsible that poverty you have courted is more easily found than the accomplishment of your wishes, and I would avoid the sight of another reduced to my condition.

"Nor is it necessary to devote the time that I did to this matter, as accident alone, without the promised key, will ever develop the mystery. If revealed by accident a few hours devoted to the subject may accomplish results which were denied to years of patient toil. Again, never, as I have done, sacrifice your own and your family's interests to what may prove an illusion. But as I have already said, when your day's work is done, and you are comfortably seated by your good fire, a short time devoted to the subject can injure no one, and may bring its reward.

"By pursuing this policy your interests will not suffer, your family will be cared for and your thoughts will not be absorbed to the exclusion of other important matters. With this admonition, I submit to my readers the papers upon which this narrative is founded.

"The first, in order, is the letter from Beale to Mr. Morriss, which will give the reader a clearer conception of all the facts connected with the case, and enable him to understand as fully as I myself do the present status of the affair. The letter is as follows:

Lynchburg, Va., January 4th, 1822.

My dear friend Morriss:

You will doubtless be surprised when you discover from a perusal of this letter, the importance of the trust confided to you, and the confidence reposed in your honor, by parties whom you have never seen and whose names you have never heard. The reasons are simple and easily told. It was imperative upon us that some one here should be selected to carry out our wishes in case of accident to ourselves, and your reputation as a man of integrity, unblemished honor, and business sagacity, influenced them to select you in place of others better known but, perhaps, not so reliable as yourself.

It was with this design that I first visited your house, two years hence, that I might judge by personal observation if your reputation was merited. To enable me the better to do so, I remained with you more than three months, and until I was fully satisfied as to your character. This visit was made by the request of my associates, and you can judge from their actions whether my report was a favorable one.

I will now give you some idea of the enterprise in which we are engaged, and the duties will be required of you in connection therewith; first assuring you, however, that your compensation for the trouble will be ample, as you have been unanimously made one of our association, and as such are entitled to share equally with the others.

Some five years since, I in connection with several friends, who, like myself, were fond of adventure, and if mixed with a little danger all the more acceptable, determined to visit the great western plains

125

and enjoy in hunting buffalo, grizzly bears, and such other game as the country would afford. This, at that time, was our sole object, and we at once proceeded to put it in execution.

On account of Indians and other dangers incident to such an undertaking, we determined to raise a party of not less than thirty individuals of good character and standing, who would be pleasant companions and financially able to encounter the expense. With this object in view, each one of us suggested the subject to his several friends and acquaintances, and in a few weeks the requisite number had signed the conditions and were admitted as members of the party. Some few refused to join us, being, doubtless, deterred by the dangers, but such men we did not want and were glad of their refusal.

The company being formed, we forthwith commenced our preparations and, early in April 1817, left old Virginia for St. Louis, Mo. where we expected to purchase the necessary outfits, procure a guide and two or three servants, and obtain such information and advice as might be beneficial hereafter. All was done as intended and we left St. Louis the 19th of May, to be absent two years our objective point being Santa Fe, which we intended to reach in the ensuing fall, and there establish ourselves in winter quarters.

After leaving St. Louis, we were advised by our guide to form a regular military organization, with a captain to be selected by the members to whom should be given sole authority to manage our affairs, and, in case of necessity, ensure united action. This was agreed to and each member of the party bound himself by a solemn obligation to obey, at all times, the orders of their captain, or, in event of refusal, to leave the company at once.

This arrangement was to remain in force for two years, or for the period of our expected absence. Tyranny, partiality, incompetence or other improper conduct on the part of the captain, was to be punished by deposing him from his office if a majority of the company desired his dismissal. All this being arranged and a set of laws framed, by which the conduct of the members was to be regulated, the election was held and resulted in choosing me as their leader.

It is not my purpose now to give you details of our wanderings, or of the pleasures or dangers encountered. All this I will reserve until we meet again, when it will be a pleasure to recall incidents that will always be fresh in my memory.

About the first of December, we reached our destination, Santa Fe, and prepared for a long and welcome rest from the fatigues of our journey. Nothing of interest occured during the winter, and of this little Mexican town we soon became heartily tired. We longed for the advent of weather which would enable us to resume our wanderings and our exhilarating pursuits.

Early in March some of our party, to vary the monotony of their lives, determined upon a short excursion for the purpose of hunting and examining the country around us. They expected to be only a few days absent, but days passed into weeks, and weeks into a month or more, before we had any tidings of the party.

We had become exceedingly uneasy and were preparing to send out scouts to trace them, if possible, when two of the party arrived and gave an explanation of their absence. It appears that when they left Santa Fe, they pursued a northerly course for some days, being successful in finding an abundance of game, which they secured, and were on the eve of returning when they discovered on their left an immense herd of buffaloes heading for a valley just perceptible in the distance. They determined to follow them, and secure as many as possible. Keeping well together, they followed their trail for two weeks or more securing many and stampeding the rest.

One day, while following them, the party encamped in a ravine some 250 or 300 miles to the north of Santa Fe and with their horses tethered were preparing their evening meal when one of the men discovered in a cleft of the rocks something that had the appearance of gold. Upon showing it to the others, it was pronounced to be gold--and much excitement was the natural consequence. Messengers were at once dispatched to inform me of the facts and request my presence with the rest of the party--and with supplies for an indefinite time.

All the pleasures and temptations which had lured them to the plains were now forgotten, and visions of boundless wealth and future grandeur were the only ideas entertained.

Upon reaching the locality I found all as it had been represented, and the excitement intense. Everyone was diligently at work with such tools and appliances as they had improvised, and quite a little pile had already accumulated. Though all were at work, there was nothing like order or method in their plans, and my first efforts were to systematize our operations and reduce everything to order.

With this object in view, an agreement was entered into to work in common, as joint partners, the accumulations of each one to be placed in a common receptacle, and each be entitled to an equal share of the whole whenever he chose to withdraw it; the whole to remain under my charge until some other disposition of it was agreed upon. Under this arrangement the work progressed favorably for eighteen months or more, and a great deal of gold had accumulated in my hands, as well as silver, which had likewise been found. Everything necessary for our purposes and for the prosecution of the work had been obtained from Santa Fe, and no trouble was experienced in procuring assistance from the Indians in our labors.

Matters went on thus until the summer of 1819, when the question of transferring our wealth to some secure place was frequently discussed. It was not considered advisable to retain so large an amount in so wild and dangerous a locality, where its very possession might endanger our lives; and to conceal it there would avail nothing, as we might at any time be forced to reveal its place of concealment.

We were in a dilemma. Some advised one plan, some another. One recommended Santa Fe as the safest place to deposit it, while others objected and advocated its shipment at once to the States, where it was ultimately to go, and where alone it would be safe. The idea seemed to prevail and it was doubtless correct, that when outside parties ascertained, as they would do, that we kept nothing on hand to tempt their cupidity, our lives would be more secure than at present.

It was finally decided that it would be best to send it to Virginia, under my charge, and there be securely buried in a cave near Buford's Tavern, in the county of Bedford, which all of us had visited, and which was considered a perfectly safe depository. This was acceptable to all, and I at once made preparations for my departure. The whole party were to accompany me for the first five hundred miles, when all but ten would return, these latter to remain with me to the end of the journey. All was carried out as arranged, and I arrived safely with my charge.

Stopping at Buford's Tavern, where we remained for a month under pretense of hunting, etc., we visited the cave but found it unfit for our purpose. It was too frequently visited by the neighboring farmers who used it as a receptacle for their sweet potatoes and other vegetables. We soon selected a better place, and to this the treasure was safely transferred.

Before leaving my companions on the plains, it was suggested that in case of an accident to ourselves, the treasure so concealed would be lost to their relatives without some provision against such a contingency. I was, therefore, instructed to select some perfectly reliable person, if such anyone could be found, who should, in the event of his proving acceptable to the party, be confided in to carry out their wishes in regard to their respective shares, and upon my return report whether I had found such a person. It was in accordance with these instructions that I visited you, made your acquaintance, was satisfied that you would suit us, and so reported.

On my return, I found the work still progressing favorably, and, by making large accessions to our force of laborers, I was ready to return last fall with an increased supply of metal, which came through safely and was deposited with the other. It was at this time I handed you the box, not disclosing the nature of the contents but asking you to keep it safely till called for." I intend writing you, however, from St. Louis and impressing upon you its importance still more forcibly.

The papers enclosed herewith will be unintelligible without the key, which will reach you in time, and will be found merely to state the contents of our depository, with its exact location, and a list of the names of our party, with their places of residence, etc.

I thought, at first, to give you their names in this letter, but reflecting that some one may read the letter and thus be enabled to impose upon you by impersonating some member of the party, have decided the present plan is best.

You will be aware from what I have written, that we are engaged in a perilous enterprise, one which promises glorious results if successful, but dangers intervene, and of the end no one can tell. We can only hope for the best, and persevere until our work is accomplished, and the sum secured for which we are striving.

As ten years must elapse before you will see this letter, you may well conclude by that time that the worst has happened and that none of us is to be numbered with the living. In such an event, you will please visit the place of deposit and secure its contents, which you will divide into thirty-one equal parts, one of these parts you are to retain as your own, freely given for your services. The other shares are to be distributed to the parties named in the accompanying paper. These legacies, so unexpectedly received, will at least serve to recall names that may still be cherished though partially forgotten.

In conclusion, my dear friend, I beg that you will not allow any false or idle punctillio to prevent your receiving and appropriating the portion assigned to yourself. It is a gift, not from myself alone but from each member of our party, and will not be out of proportion to the services required of you.

I trust, my dear Mr. Morriss, that we may meet many times in the future, but if the Fates forbid, with my last communication, I would assure you of the entire respect and confidence of

Your friend,<br>Tho. Jeff. Beale.

"The second letter in the box is as follows:

Lynchburg, Va., January 5th, 1822.

Dear Mr. Morriss:

You will find in one of the papers, written in cipher, the names of all my associates, and opposite to the name of each one will be found the names and residences of relatives and others to whom they devise their respective portions.

From this you will be enabled to carry out the wishes of all by distributing the portion of each to the parties designated. This will not be difficult as their residences are given, and they can easily be found.

T. J. B.

"The two letters given above were all the box contained that were intelligible. The others consisted of papers closely covered with figures, which were of course, unmeaning until they could be deciphered. To do this was the task to which I now devoted myself, and with but partial success, that is, as to deciphering paper marked 'No. 2', to be described later on.

"The three ciphers are given below, the one marked No. 1', describing the exact locality of the vault where the treasure is buried; the one marked 'No. 2', stating the contents of the vault; and paper marked 'No. 3', stating the names and addresses of the persons involved:

"No. 1"

71, 194, 38, 1701, 89, 76, 11, 83, 1629, 48, 94, 63, 132, 16, 111' 95, 84, 341, 975, 14, 40, 64, 27, 81, 139, 213, 63, 90, 1120, 8, 15, 3' 126, 2018, 40, 74, 758, 485, 604, 230, 436, 664, 582, 150, 251, 284, 308, 231, 124' 211, 486, 225, 401, 370' 11, 101, 305, 139 (130?)' 189, 17' 33, 88, 208, 193, 145, 1, 94, 73, 416, 918, 263, 28, 500, 538, 356, 117, 136, 219, 27, 176' 130, 10, 460, 25, 485, 18, 436, 65, 84, 200, 283, 118, 320, 138' 36, 416, 280, 15, 71, 224, 961, 44, 16, 401, 39, 88, 61, 304, 12, 21, 24, 283, 134, 92, 63, 246, 486, 682, 7' 219, 184, 360, 780, 18, 64, 463, 474, 131, 160, 79, 73, 440, 95, 18, 64, 581, 34, 69, 128, 367, 460, 17, 81, 12, 103, 820, 62, 116' 97, 103, 862, 70, 60, 1317, 471, 540, 208, 121, 890, 346, 36, 150, 59, 568, 614, 13, 120' 63' 219, 812, 2160, 1780, 99, 35, 18, 21, 136, 872, 15, 28, 170, 88, 4' 30, 44, 112, 18, 147, 436, 195, 320, 37, 122, 113, 6, 140, 8, 120, 305, 42, 58, 461, 44, 106, 301, 13, 408, 680, 93, 86, 116, 530, 82, 568, 9, 102, 38, 416, 89, 71, 216, 728, 965, 818, 2, 38, 121, 195, 14, 326, 148, 234, 18, 55, 131, 234, 361, 824, 5' 81, 623, 48, 961, 19, 26, 33, 10, 1101' 365, 92, 88, 181, 275, 346, 201, 206, 86, 36, 219, 320, 829, 840, 68, 326, 19, 48, 122, 85, 216, 284, 919, 861, 326, 985, 233, 64, 68, 232, 431, 431, 960, 50, 29, 81, 216, 321, 603, 14, 612, 81, 360, 36, 51, 62, 194, 78, 60, 200, 314, 676, 112' 4' 28, 18, 61, 136, 247, 819, 921, 1060, 464, 895, 10, 6' 66, 119, 38, 41, 49, 602,

423, 962, 302, 294, 875, 78, 14, 23, 111, 109, 62, 31, 501, 823, 216, 280, 34' 24, 150, 1000, 162, 286, 19, 21, 17, 340, 19, 242, 31, 86, 234, 140, 607, 115, 33, 191, 67, 104, 86, 52, 88, 16, 80, 121, 67, 95, 122, 216, 548, 96, 11, 201, 77, 364, 218, 65, 667, 890, 236, 154, 211, 10, 98, 34, 119, 56, 216, 119, 71, 218, 1164, 1496, 1817, 51, 39, 210, 36, 3, 19, 540, 232, 22, 141, 617, 84, 290, 80, 46, 207, 411, 150, 29, 38, 46, 172, 85, 194, 36, 261, 543, 897, 624, 18, 212, 416, 127, 931, 19, 4, 63, 96, 12, 101, 418, 16, 140, 230, 460, 538, 19, 27, 88, 612, 1431, 90, 716, 275, 74, 83, 11, 426, 89, 72, 84, 1300, 1706, 814, 221, 132, 40, 102, 34, 858, 975, 1101, 84, 16, 79, 23, 16, 81, 122, 324, 403, 912, 227, 936, 447, 55, 86, 34, 43, 212, 107, 96, 314, 264, 1065, 323, 428, 601, 203, 124, 95, 216, 814, 2906, 654, 820, 2, 301, 112, 176, 213, 71, 87' 96, 202, 35, 10, 2, 41, 17' 84, 221, 736, 820, 214, 11, 60, 760.

"No.2."

115, 73, 24, 818, 37, 52, 49, 17, 31, 62, 657, 22, 7, 15, 140, 47, 29, 107, 79, 84, 56, 238, 10, 26, 822, 5, 195, 308, 85, 52, 159, 136, 59, 210, 36, 9' 46, 316, 543, 122, 106, 95, 53, 58, 2, 42, 7, 35, 122, 53' 31, 82, 77, 250, 195, 56, 96, 118, 71, 140, 287, 28, 353, 37, 994, 65, 147, 818, 24, 3, 8' 12, 47, 43, 59, 818, 45, 316, 101, 41, 78, 154, 994, 122, 138, 190, 16, 77, 49, 102, 57, 72, 34, 73, 85, 35, 371, 59, 195, 81, 92, 190, 106, 273, 60, 394, 629, 270, 219, 106, 388, 287, 63, 3, 6, 190, 122, 43, 233, 400, 106, 290, 314, 47, 48, 81, 96, 26, 115, 92, 157, 190, 110, 77, 85, 196, 46, 10, 113, 140, 353, 48, 120, 106, 2, 616, 61, 420, 822, 29, 125, 14, 20, 37, 105, 28, 248, 16, 158, 7, 35, 19, 301, 125, 110, 496, 287' 98, 117' 520, 62, 51, 219, 37' 113, 140, 818, 138, 549, 8, 44, 287, 388, 117, 18, 79, 344, 34, 20, 59, 520, 557, 107, 612, 219, 37, 66, 154, 41, 20, 50, 6, 584, 122, 154, 248, 110, 61, 52, 33, 30, 5, 38, 8, 14, 84, 57' 549, 216, 115, 71, 29, 85, 63, 43, 131, 29, 138, 47, 73, 238, 549, 52, 53' 79, 118, 51, 44, 63, 195, 12, 238, 112, 3' 49, 79, 353, 105, 56, 371, 566, 210, 515, 125, 360, 133, 143, 101, 15, 284, 549, 252, 14, 204, 140, 344, 26, 822, 138' 115, 48, 73, 34, 204, 316,

616, 63, 219, 7' 52, 150, 44, 52, 16, 40, 37, 157, 818, 37, 121, 12, 95, 10, 15, 35, 12, 131, 62, 115, 102, 818, 49, 53, 135, 138, 30, 31, 62, 67, 41, 85, 63, 10, 106, 818, 138' 8, 113, 20, 32, 33, 37, 353, 287, 140, 47, 85, so, 37, 49, 47, 64, 6, 7, 71, 33, 4, 43, 47, 63, 1, 27, 609, 207, 229, 15, 190, 246, 85, 94, 520, 2, 270, 20, 39, 7, 33, 44, 22, 40, 7, 10, 3, 822, 106, 44, 496, 229, 353, 210, 199, 31, 10, 38, 140, 297, 61, 612, 320, 302, 676, 287, 2, 44, 33, 32, 520, 557, 10, 6, 250, 566, 246, 53, 37, 52, 83, 47, 320, 38 (39?), 33, 818, 7, 44, 30, 31, 250, 10, 15, 35, 106, 159, 113, 31, 102, 406, 229, 549, 320, 29, 66, 33, 101, 818, 138, 301, 316, 353, 320, 219, 37, 52, 28, 549, 320, 33, 8, 46, 107, 50, 822, 7, 2, 113, 73, 16, 125, 11, 110, 67, 102, 818, 33, 59, 81, 157, 38, 43, 590, 138, 19, 85, 400, 38, 43, 77, 14, 27, 8' 47, 138, 63, 140, 44, 35, 22, 176, 106, 250, 314, 216, 2, 10, 7, 994' 4, 20, 25, 44, 48, 7, 26, 46, 110, 229, 818, 190, 34, 112' 147' 44, 110' 121, 125, 96, 41, 51, so, 140, 56, 47, 152, 549, 63, 818, 28, 42, 250 138, 591, 98, 653, 32, 107, 140, 112, 26, 85, 138, 549, 50, 20, 125, 371, 38, 36, 10, 52, 118' 136, 102, 420, 150, 112, 71, 14, 20, 7, 24, 18, 12, 818, 37, 67,110, 62, 33, 21, 95, 219, 520, 102, 822, 30, 83, 84, 305, 629, 15, 2, 10, 8, 219, 106, 353, 105, 106, 60, 242, 72, 8, 50, 204, 184, 112, 125, 549, 65, 106, 818, 190, 96, 110, 16, 73, 33, 818, 150, 409, 400, 50, 154, 285, 96, 106, 316, 270, 204, 101, 822, 400, 8, 44, 37' 52, 40, 240, 34, 204, 38, 16, 46, 47' 85, 24, 44, 15, 64, 73, 38, 818, 85, 78, 110, 33, 420, 515, 53, 37, 38, 22, 31, 10, 110, 106, 101, 140, 15, 38, 3, 5, 44, 7, 98, 287, 135, 150, 96, 33, 84, 125, 818, 190, 96, 520, 118, 459, 370, 653, 466, 106, 41, 107, 612, 219, 275, 30, 150, 105, 49, 53, 287' 250, 207' 134, 7' 53, 12, 47, 85, 63, 138, 110, 21, 112, 140, 495, 496, 515, 14, 73, 85, 584, 994, 150, 199, 16, 42, 5, 4, 25, 42, 8, 16, 822, 125, 159, 32, 204, 612, 818, 81, 95, 405, 41, 609, 136, 14, 20, 28, 26, 353, 302, 246, 8, 131, 159, 140, 84, 440, 42, 16, 822, 40, 67' 101, 102, 193, 138, 204, 51, 63, 240, 549, 122, 8, 10, 63, 140, 47' 48, 140, 288.

"No. 3"

317, 8' 92' 73, 112' 89, 67, 318, 28, 96, 107, 41, 631, 78, 146,
397, 118, 98, 114, 246, 348, 116' 74, 88, 12, 65, 32, 14, 81, 19,
76, 121, 216, 85, 33, 66, 15' 108, 68, 77, 43, 24, 122, 96, 117'
36, 211, 301, 15, 44, 11, 46, 89, 18, 136' 68, 317, 28, 90, 82,
304, 71, 43, 221, 198, 176, 310, 319, 81, 99, 264, 380, 56, 37,
319, 2, 44, 53, 28, 44, 75, 98, 102, 37, 85, 107, 117' 64, 88,
136' 48, 151, 99, 175, 89, 315, 326, 78, 96, 214, 218, 311'
43, 89, 51, 90, 75, 128, 96, 33, 28, 103, 84, 65, 26, 41, 246,
84, 270, 98, 116, 32, 59, 74, 66, 69, 240, 15, 8, 121, 20, 77,
89, 31, 11, 106, 81, 191, 224, 328, 18, 75, 52, 82, 117, 201, 39,
23, 217, 27, 21, 84, 35, 54, 109, 128, 49, 77, 88, 1, 81, 217,
64, 55, 83, 116, 251, 269, 311, 96, 54, 32, 120, 18, 132, 102,
219, 211, 84, 150, 219, 275, 312, 64, 10, 106, 87, 75, 47, 21,
29, 37, 81, 44, 18, 126, 115, 132, 160, 181, 203, 76, 81, 299,
314, 337, 351, 96, 11, 28, 97, 318, 238, 106, 24, 93, 3, 19, 17,
26, 60, 73, 88, 14, 126, 138, 234, 286, 297, 321, 365, 264, 19,
22, 84, 56, 107, 98, 123' 111, 214, 136, 7' 33, 45, 40, 13, 28,
46, 42, 107, 196, 227, 344, 198, 203, 247, 116, 19, 8' 212, 230,
31, 6, 328, 65, 48, 52, 59, 41, 122, 33, 117' 11, 18, 25, 71, 36,
45, 83, 76, 89, 92, 31, 65, 70, 83, 96, 27, 33, 44, 50, 61, 24,
112, 136, 149, 176, 180, 194, 143, 171, 205, 296, 87, 12, 44, 51,
89, 98, 34, 41, 208, 173, 66, 9, 35, 16, 95, 8, 113, 175, 90, 56,
203, 19, 177, 183, 206, 157, 200, 218, 260, 291, 305, 618, 951,
320, 18, 124, 78, 65, 19, 32, 124, 48, 53, 57, 84, 96, 207, 244,
66, 82, 119, 71, 11, 86, 77' 213, 54, 82, 316, 245, 303, 86, 97'
106, 212, 18, 37, 15, 81, 89, 16, 7, 81, 39, 96, 14, 43, 216,
118, 29, 55, 109, 136, 172, 213, 64, 8, 227' 304, 611, 221, 364,
819, 375, 128, 296, 11, 18, 53, 76, 10, 15, 23, 19, 71, 84,
120, 134, 66, 73, 89, 96, 230, 48, 77, 26, 101, 127, 936, 218,
439, 178, 171, 61, 226, 313, 215, 102, 18, 167' 262, 114, 218,
66, 59, 48, 27' 19, 13, 82, 48, 162, 119, 34, 127' 139, 34, 128,
129, 74, 63, 120, 11, 54, 61, 73, 92, 180, 66, 75, 101, 124, 265,
89, 96, 126, 274, 896, 917' 434, 461, 235, 890, 312, 413, 328,
381, 96, 105, 217, 66, 118, 22, 77, 64, 42, 12, 7, 55, 24, 83,
67, 97,109,121,135,181,203,219,228, 256, 21, 34, 77, 319,
374, 382, 675, 684, 717, 864, 203, 4, 18, 92, 16, 63, 82, 22, 46,

55, 69, 74, 112, 135, 186, 175, 119, 213, 416, 312, 343, 264,
119, 186, 218, 343, 417, 845, 951, 124, 209, 49, 617, 856 (356?),
924, 936, 72, 19, 29, 11, 35, 42, 40, 66, 85, 94, 112, 65, 82,
115, 119, 236, 244, 186, 172, 112, 85, 6, 56, 38, 44, 85, 72, 32,
47, 73, 96(?), 124,217,314,319,221,644,817,821,934,922,
416, 975, 10, 22, 18, 46, 137' 181, 101, 39, 86, 103, 116, 138,
164, 212, 218, 296, 815, 380 (390?), 412, 460, 495, 675, 820,
952.

"The papers given above were all that were contained in the box, except two or three of an unimportant character, and having no connection whatever with the subject in hand. They were carefully copied, and as carefully compared with the originals, and no error is believed to exist.

"Complete in themselves, they are now respectfully submitted to the public with the hope that all that is dark in them may receive light, and that the treasure, amounting, as I figure it at this time, to more than three-quarters of a million dollars, which has rested so long unproductive of good, in the hands of a proper person may eventually accomplish its mission.

"To enable my readers to understand the paper "No. 2", the only one I was ever able to decipher, I herewith give the Declaration of Independence, with the words numbered consecutively, by the assistance of which the paper's hidden meaning was made plain:

IN CONGRESS JULY 4, 1776

A Declaration by the Representatives of the UNITED STATES OF
AMERICA in General Congress Assembled.

When, in the course of human events, it becomes necessary for one
people to dissolve the political bands which have connected them with
another, and to assume among the powers of the earth the separate and
equal station to which the Laws of Nature and of Nature's God entitle
them a decent respect to the opinions of mankind requires that they
should declare the causes which impel them to the separation.

We hold these truths to be self-evident; that all men are created
equal, that they are endowed by their Creator with certain unalienable

96      97  98    99    100 101 102      103 104 105   106
rights; that among these are Life, Liberty, and the pursuit of

107         108 109 110   111   112   113         114
Happiness.  That to secure these rights Governments are

115        116  117 118      119   120 121    122 123 124
instituted among men, deriving their just powers from the consent

125 126 127      128 129      130 131 132 133      134
of the governed.  That whenever any Form of Government becomes

135        136 137   138 139 140 141   142 143 144 145    146
destructive of these ends, it  is the   right of  the People to

147   148 149 150   151  152 153  154       155 156
alter or  to abolish it  and  to  institute new Government,

157    158 159      160 161 162      163 164      165 166
laying its foundation on such principles and organizing its powers

167 168  169  170 171  172  173   174 175   176  177 178
in  such form  as  to  them shall seem most likely to effect

179    180   181 182        183      184      185 186    187
their Safety and Happiness.  Prudence, indeed, will dictate that

188        189  190      191   192 193 194    195  196 197
Governments long established should not be  changed for light and

198        199   200 201      202 203      204  205  206
transient causes; and accordingly, all experience hath shown that

207    208 209 210    211 212   213   214   215 216
mankind are more disposed to suffer, while evils are sufferable,

217 218 219   220      221 222      223 224 225 226   227
than  to right themselves by  abolishing the forms to which they

228 229      230 231 232 233 234 235 236    237 238
are accustomed. But, when a   long train of  abuses and usurpations,

239    240      241 242 243   244      245 246   247 248
pursuing invariably the same Object, evinces a   design to reduce

249 250  251    252      253 254 255 256   257 258 259
them under absolute Despotism, it  is  their right, it  is  their

260 261 262 263 264 265      266 267 268    269 270
duty to throw off such Government, and  to  provide new Guards

271 272   273    274          275  276 277  278 279
for their future security.  --Such has been the patient

280         281 282  283        284  285  286 287 288  289
sufferance of   these Colonies; and  such  is now the necessity

which contrains them to alter their former Systems of Government.

      300  301    302 303  304    305  306 307   308     309 310  311
      The history of  the present King  of Great Britain  is  a history

312 313     314      315 316        317  318   319  320
of  repeated injuries and usurpations, all having  in direct

321    322 323        324 325 326      327      328  329    330
object the establishment of  an  absolute Tyranny over these States.

331 332    333  334 335  336  337      338 339  340    341
To  prove this, let Facts be  submitted to  a   candid world:

      342 343 344    345 346    347 348   349  350  351       352
      He  has refused his Assent to  Laws, the most wholesome and

353         354 355 356    357
necessary for the public good.

      358  359 360        361 362      363 364  365  366 367
      He   has forbidden his Governors  to pass Laws  of immediate

368  369    370      371    372      373 374   375      376
and pressing importance, unless suspended  in their operation till

377 378    379   380 381     382 383 384  385      386 387
his Assent should be obtained; and when  so suspended  he has

388    389      390 391   392 393
utterly neglected  to attend  to them.

      394 395 396    397 398  399   400  401 402 403
      He  has refused  to pass other Laws for the accommodation

404 405  406      407  408   409   410   411   412    413
of large districts  of people, unless those people would relinquish

414 415   416 417        418 419  420        421  422
the right  of Representation  in the Legislature,   a right

423       424 425 426  427      428 429    430
inestimable  to them and formidable to Tyrants only.

      431 432 433   434      435      436    437 438   439
      He  has called together legislative bodies  at places unusual,

440                 441 442       443  444  445        446   447   448
uncomfortable, and distant from the depository  of their Public

449       450 451   452    453     454  455        456  457     458
Records for the sole purpose  of fatiguing them into compliance

459   460 461
with his measures.

        462 463 464        465              466    467         468
        He  has dissolved Representative Houses repeatedly, for

469       470   471  472       473    474     475 476  477    478
opposing with manly firmness his invasions  on the rights  of

479 480
the people.

        481 482 483       484 485 486  487    488    489   490
        He  has refused for   a long time, after such dissolutions,

491  492  493    494 495  496    497        498  499        500
to cause others  to  be elected; whereby the Legislative Powers,

501       502 503          504  505     506 507  508   509 510
incapable  of Annihilation, have returned  to the People  at large

511  512  513       514  515   516       517 518  519       520
for their exercise; the State remaining,  in the meantime, exposed

521 522 523  524    525 526       527   528     529 530        531
to all the dangers  of invasion from without and convulsions within.

        532 533 534       535 536     537 538        539 540
        He  has endeavored  to prevent the population  of these
541       542 543 544    545          546 547  548  549
States;  for that purpose obstructing the Laws for Naturalization

550 551       552       553 554   555    556 557       558
of  Foreigners; refusing  to pass others  to encourage their

559       560    561 562     563  564     565  566  567
migration hither and raising the conditions  of new Appropriations

568 569
of Lands.

        570 571 572       573 574        575 576       577 578
        He  has obstructed the Administration  of Justice,  by refusing

579 580    581  582 583  584       585       586
his Assent  to Laws for establishing Judiciary Powers.

587   588 589  590      591         592 593  594  595       596 597
He    has made Judges dependent on  his  Will alone , for the

598    599 600   601       602 603 604   605  606    607 608
tenure of  their offices, and the amount and payment of  their

609
salaries.

610 611  612     613  614       615 616 617       618 619  620
He  has erected  a  multitude of  New Offices, and sent hither

621    622 623       624  625  626 627      628 629 630 631   632
swarms of  Officers to harass our People, and eat out their substance.

633 634 635  636    637  638 639    640 641    642       643
He  has kept among  us,  in times of  peace, Standing Armies,

644    645 646    647 648 649
without the consent of  our legislature.

650 651  652    653  654    655  656     657        658
He  has affected  to  render the Military independent of

659  660     661 662  663  664
and superior to  the Civil Power.

665 666  667    668  669    670 671     672 673 674
He  has combined with others to  subject  us  to  a

675         676    677 678  679       680  681       682
jurisdiction foreign to  our constitution and unacknowledged by

683 684   685    686 687   688 689   690  691 692     693
our laws; giving his assent  to their acts of  pretended legislation.

694 695       696   697   698 699 700    701  702
For quartering large bodies of armed troops among  us.

703   704      705   706 707 708 709    710 711
For protecting them, by   a  mock Trial, from Punishment

712 713 714     715  716   717  718    719 720  721       722
for any Murders which they should commit  on the Inhabitants of

723   724
these States.

725   726   727 728 729   730  731 732   733 734 735
For cutting off our Trade with all parts of  the world.

736 737      738   739 740 741     742 743
For imposing taxes on  us  without our Consent.

744 745      746 747 748  749  750 751 752      753 754
For depriving us,  in  many cases, of the benefits  of Trial

755  756
by  Jury.

757 758           759 760    761 762  763 764 765    766
For transporting us  beyond Seas to  be  tried for  pretended

767
offences.

768 769      770 771   772   773 774     775 776 777
For abolishing the free System of  English Laws  in  a

778        779      780      781   782 783      784
neighboring Province, establishing therein an  Arbitrary government,

785 786      787 788      789 790 791 792    793 794 795  796
and enlarging  its Boundaries so  as  to  render it  at  once an

797    798 799 800      801  802      803  804 805    806
example and fit instrument for introducing the same absolute rule

807 808   809
in  these Colonies.

810 811    812 813 814    815        816 817 818
For taking away our Charter, abolishing our most valuable

819  820 821    822        823 824   825 826 827
Laws, and altering fundamentally the Forms of  our Governments.

828  829      830 831 832      833 834      835
For suspending our own Legislature, and declaring themselves

836      837 838  839 840    841 842 843 844 845  846
invested with Power to legislate for us  in  all cases whatsoever.

847 848 849    850      851  852 853    854 855 856 857
He  has abdicated Government here, by declaring us  out of  his

858      859 860  861  862  863
protection, and waging War against us.

864 865 866    867 868  869    870 871  872  873 874
He  has plundered our seas, ravaged our Coasts, burnt our towns,

1023 1024   1025 1026      1027 1028 1029   1030 1031  1032
  A   Prince whose character  is  thus marked  by  every  act

1033   1034 1035  1036 1037   1038 1039  1040 1041 1042 1043
which  may define   a  tyrant  is  unfit  to   be  the  ruler

1044 1045 1046  1047
of   a   free people.

     1048 1049  1050 1051 1052   1053  1054      1055 1056  1057
     Nor  have  We  been wanting  in  attentions  to  our  British

1058      1059  1060  1061  1062 1063 1064 1065 1066 1067 1068
brethren. We   have warned them from time  to  time  of  attempts

1069 1070 1071      1072  1073  1074 1075         1076
by their legislature  to  extend  an  unwarrantable jurisdiction

1077  1078
over  us.

     1079 1080 1081     1082 1083 1084 1085       1086 1087
     We   have reminded them  of  the  circumstances  of  our

1088      1089  1090     1091  1092 1093  1094     1095 1096
emigration and settlement here.  We   have appealed  to  their

1097    1098   1099 1100      1101 1102 1103  1104   1105 1106
native justice and magnanimity, and  we   have conjured them  by

1107 1108 1109 1110  1111   1112    1113  1114    1115   1116
the  ties  of   our  common kindred  to   disavow these usurpations,

1117  1118   1119      1120     1121 1122       1123   1124
which would inevitably interrupt our  connections and  correspondence.

1125  1126 1127 1128  1129 1130 1131  1132 1133  1134   1125 1136
They, too, have been deaf  to   the voice  of  justice  and  of

1137
consanguinity.

     1138 1139  1140      1141      1142 1143 1144      1145
     We   must, therefore, acquiesce in   the  necessity which

1146      1147  1148      1149 1150 1151  1152 1153 1154 1155
denounces our  Separation, and  hold them,  as  we   hold the

1156 1157 1158     1159     1160 1161 1162 1163   1164
rest  of  mankind; Enemies  in  War;  in  Peace, Friends.

1165  1166     1167  1168            1169 1170  1171   1172
We,  therefore, the  Representatives  of  the  United States

1173 1174   1175  1176   1177     1178        1179     1180  1181
of America,  in  General Congress Assembled, appealing  to  the

1182     1183 1184 1185  1186  1187 1188  1189    1190  1191
Supreme Judge  of  the  world  for  the  rectitude  of  our

1192     1193  1194 1195 1196  1197 1198 1199     1200 1201
intentions,  do,  in the  Name  and  by  Authority of  the

1202 1203   1204 1205 1206     1207     1208     1209  1210
good People  of  these Colonies, solemnly publish  and  declare

1211 1212  1213   1214     1215  1216 1217 1218  1219 1220 1221
that these United Colonies  are,  and  of Right ought  to   be,

1222 1223  1224       1225     1226 1227 1228  1229     1230 1231
Free and  Independent States; that they  are Absolved from  all

1232      1233 1234  1235     1236   1237 1238 1239 1240
Allegiance  to   the  British Crown,  and that  all political

1241      1242     1243 1244  1245 1246  1247    1248  1249
connection between them  and  the  State  of   Great Britain

1250 1251 1252  1253 1254 1255    1256       1257 1258   1259
is,  and  ought  to  be,  totally dissolved;  and  that,  as

1260 1261 1262      1263     1264 1265 1266 1267  1268 1269 1270
Free  and Independent States, they have full Power  to  levy War,

1271     1272  1273    1274      1275      1276      1277 1278
conclude Peace, contract Alliances, establish Commerce,  and  to

1279 1280 1281  1282 1283 1284   1285  1286       1287  1288
do   all  other Acts and  Things which Independent States may

1289 1290  1291
of  right  do.

1292 1293 1294  1925   1296 1297  1298      1299 1300  1301
And  for   the  support of this Declaration, with a     firm

1302     1303 1304 1305     1306 1307  1308      1309 1310
reliance on   the  Protection  of  Divine Providence  we  mutually

```
1311      1312 1313 1314 1315 1316    1317 1318      1319   1320
pledge   to  each other our  Lives,  our Fortunes, and   our

1321    1322
sacred Honor.
```

"I furnish herewith a translation of Paper No. 2, indicating of what the treasure consists, based upon the use of the Declaration of Independence as the key:

```
115  73 24 818 37  52 49  17  31  62  657  22  7  15  140  47
I    h  a  v   e   d  e    p   o   s   i    t   e  d  i    n

29  107 79 84 56 238 10 26 822 5 195
t   h   e  C  o  u   n  t  y   o f

308  85 52 159 136 49 210 36 0 46 316 543
B    e  d  f   o   r  d   a  b o  u   t

122 106 95 53 58 2 42 7 35 122 52 31 82
f   o   u  r  m  i l  e s  f   r  o  m

77 250 195 56 96 118 71 140 187 28 353
B  u   f   o  r  d   s  i   n   a  n

37 994 65 147 818 24 3 8 12 47  43 59  818 45 316 101 41
e  x   c  a   v   a  t i o  n   o  r   v   a  u   l   t

78 154 994 122 138 190 16 77 49 102 57 72  34 73 85
s  i   x   f   e   e   t  b  e  l   o  w   t  h  e

35 371 59 195 81 92 190 106 273 60 394 629
s  u   r  f   a  c  e   o   f   t  h   e

270 219 106 388 287 63 3 6 190
g   r   o   u   n   d  t h e

122 43 233 400 106 290 314 47 48 81 96 26 115 92 157 190 110
f   o  l   l   o   w   i   n  g  a  r  t  i   c  l   e   s

77 85 196 46 10 113 140 353 48 120 106 2 616 61 420 822
b  e  l   o  n  g   i   n   g  j   o   i n  t   l  y

29 125 14 20 37 105 28 248 16 158 7 35 19 301 125 110 496
t  o   t  h  e  p   a  r   t  i   e s  w  h   o   s   e
```

144

287 98 117 520 62  51 219 37  113 140 818 138 549  8 44
n a m e s a r e g i v e n  i n

287 388 117 18 79 344  34 20 59 520 557
n u m b e r  t h r e e

107 612 219 37 66 154 42 10
h e r e w i t h.

50 6 584  122 154 248 110 61  52 33 30 5 38 8 14
T h e  f i r s t  d e p o s i t

84 57 549 216 115 71 29 85 63  43 131  29 138 47
c o n s i s t e d  o f  t e n

73 238 549 52 53 79 118  51 44 63  195 12 238 112 3 49 79 353
h u n d r e d  a n d  f o u r t e e n

105 56 371 566 120 515  125 360  133 143 101 15  284 549 252
p o u n d s  o f  g o l d  a n d

14 204 140 344 26 822  138 115 48 73 34
t h i r t y  e i g h t

204 316 616 63 219 7 52  150 44 52  16 40 37 157 818 37
h u n d r e d a n d t w e l v e

121 12 95 10 15 35  12 131  62 115 102 818 49 53
p o u n d s o f s i l v e r

135 138 30 31 62 67 41 85 63  10 106 818
d e p o s i t e d N o v.

138 8 113 20 32 33 37 353  287 140 47 85 50 37 49 47
e i g h t e e n  n i n e t e e n.

64 6 7  71 33 4 43 47 63  1 27 609  207 229 15 190
T h e  s e c o n d w a s  m a d e

246 85 94  520 2 270 20 39 7 33 44  22 40 7 10 3 822 106 44 496
D e c. e i g h t e e n t w e n t y - o n e

229 353 210  199 31 10 38 140 297 61 612 320  302 676
a n d  c o n s i s t e d  o f

287 2 44 33 32 520 557 10  6 250 566 246 53 37 52  83 47 320
n i n e t e e n h u n d r e d  a n d

38 33 818 7 44  30 31 250 10 15 35  106 159  113 31 102 406
s e v e n p o u n d s o f  g o l d

229 549 320  29 66 33 101 818 138  301 316 353 320 219 37 52
a     n     d  t  w  e  l   v   e   h   u   n   d   r   e  d

28 549 320  33 8 49 107 50 822  7 2 113 73 16  125 11
a    n    d  e  i  g   h  t  y   e i  g   h  t    o  f

110 67 102 818 33 59  81 157 38 43  590 138 19 85 400 38
s   i  l   v   e  r;  a  l   a  o    j   e   w  e  l   s

43 77 14 27 8 47 138 63  140 44  33 22  176 106 250 314 216
o  b  t  a  i n  e   d   i   n   S  t.   L   o   u   i   s

2 10  7 994 4 20 25 44 48 7  26 46  110 229 818 190
i n    e x  c  h  a  n  g  e  t  o   s   a   v   e

34 112 147 44 110 121 125 96 41 51 50 149 56 47  152 549 63
t  r   a   n  s   p   o   r  t  a  t  i   o  n    a   n   d

818 28 42 250 138 591  98 653  32 107 140 112 26 85 138 549
v   a  l  u   e   d     a  t    t  h   i   r   t  e  e   n

50 20 125 371 38 36 10 52  118 136 102 420 150 112 71
t  h  o   u   s  a  n  d   d   o   l   l   a   r   s.

14 20 7  24 18 13 818 37  67 110  62 33 21 95 219 520 102 822
T  h  e  a  b  o  v   e   i  s    s  e  c  u  r  e   l   y

30 83 84 305 620 15  2 10  8 219 106 353  105 106 60 242
p  a  c  k   e   d   i n   i r   o   n     p   o   t  s

72 8 50 204  184 112 125 549  65 106 818 190 96 110
w  i t  h    i   r   o   n     c  o   v   e   r  s.

16 73 53  818 150 409 400 50  154 285
T  h  e   v   a   u   l   t   i   s

96 106 316 270 204 101 822  400 8 44 37 52  40 240 34 204
r  o   u   g   h   l   y    l   i n  e  d   w  i   t  h

38 16 46 47 85  24 44 15  64 73 138  818 85 78 110 33 420 515
s  t  o  n  e   a  n  d   t  h  e    v   e  s  s   e  l   s

53 37 38 22  31 10  110 106 101 140 15  38 3 5 44 7
r  e  s  t   o  n   s   o   l   i   d   s  t o n  e,

98 287 135  150 96 33  84 125 818 190 96 520 118
a  n   d    a   r  e   c  o   v   e   r  e   d

459 370 653 466  106 41 107 612 219 275
w   i   t   h    o   t  h   e   r   s.

```
30 150 105 49 53   287 250 207 134 7 53   12 47 85
P   a   p   e  r    n   u   m   b   e r    o  n  e

63 138 110 21 112 140 495 496 515   14 73 85
d  e   s   c  r   i   b   e   s     t  h  e

584 994 150 199 16   42 5 4 25 42 8 16 822   125 159
e   x   a   c   t    l  o c a  l  i t  y     o   f

32 204 612   818 81 95 405 41   609 136   14 20 28 26
t  h   t     v   a  u  l   t,   s   o     t  h  a  t

353 302   246 8 131 159 140 84 440 42 16 822   40 67 101 102
n   o     d   i f   f   i   c  u   l  t  y     w  i  l   l

193 138   204 51 63   240 549   122 8 10 63 140 47 48   140 288.
b   e     h   a  d    i   n     f   i n d  i   n   g  i    t.
```

“In preparing his cipher No. 2, Beale used the initial letter of each numbered word refered to, except,

Word 822, fundamentally, he used the final letter, y.

Word 994, sexes, he used the medial letter, x.

Word 95, inalienable is spelled by Thomas Jefferson with a

“u”, so that Beale properly found a word in the

**Declaration of Independence beginning with “u”.**

“In conclusion, it may not be inappropriate to say a few words regarding myself: In consequence of the time lost in the above investigation, I have been reduced from comparative affluence to absolute penury, entailing suffering upon those it was my duty to protect; and this, too, in spite of their remonstrances. My eyes were at last opened to their condition, and I resolved to sever at once, and forever, all connection with the affair, and retrieve, if possible, my errors. To do this, and as the best means of placing temptation beyond my reach, determined to make public the whole matter, and shift from my shoulders my responsibility to Mr. Morriss.

“I anticipate for these papers a large circulation, and, to avoid the multitude of letters with which I should be assailed, from all sections ·Of the Union, propounding all sorts of questions and requiring answers which, if attended to, would absorb my entire time, and only change the character of my work, I have decided upon withdrawing my name from the publication, after assuring all interested that I have given all that I know of the matter, and that I cannot add one word to the statements herein contained.

"The gentlemen whom I have selected as my agent to publish and circulate these papers, was well known to Mr. Morriss; it was at his house that Mrs. Morriss died, and he would have been one of the beneficiaries in the event of my success. Like everyone else, he was ignorant of this episode in Mr. Morriss' career until the manuscript was placed in his hands.

"Trusting that he will be benefitted by the arrangement, which I know would have met the approval of Mr. Morriss, I have left the whole subject to his sole management and charge. All business communications should be addressed to him. It is needless to say that I shall await with much anxiety the development of the mystery."

# AUTHOR'S RESEARCH

Who was Beall of the Beall treasure? Was he, in fact, Thomas Jefferson Beall? Consider the following:

The key letter, the author found in the attic Bible bore the signature Thomas Jefferson Beall.

The following genealogy shows Beall's roots began with the immigrant Alexander Beall, Washington County, PA. (Ref: **Genealogy for the Beall Families in the United States of America),** located at the Library State Historical Society of Missouri, Franklin, Missouri Uncle Nell told the author that Thomas
Jefferson Beall had five older brothers, but he was closer to Uncle Nell's grandfather, Eben Nelms.

The Beall Genealogy shows Colmore Beall b 1760, d 1840, had six (6) sons. Thomas Beall was the youngest. In this genealogy there is no marriage record or death record for Thomas Beall; which further supports what Uncle Nell's statements regarding Thomas J. Beall.

The name "Captain Thos. **J.** Beall, Harper's Ferry, Common passenger," was listed on the muster roll of the ship SYRIA, **in** 1816. The muster roll appears on page 248 (Ref. **Gold in the Blue Ridge** by P.B. Innis and Walter Dean Innis.

References to Captain Beall are on pages 31 and 34 of The **Journal from Boston to the Western Countrv, and, The Journal Down the Ohio and Mississippi Rivers to New Orleans** by William Richardson. (Ref. **Gold in the Blue Ridge** by Innis and Innis)

The newspaper **Missouri Gazette,** March 31, 1820, published a list of the names of letters being held by the post office in Franklin County, MO. The name "Beall, Thomas" was listed, as were: "Buford, William, Hart and Miles."

# BIBLIOGRAPHY

The works listed have been included to provide sources of interest to the reader. The writings have been of great value in preparing this work.

1. **A Place Apart - A Brief History of the Early Williamson Road and North Roanoke Valley Residents and Places,** Helen R. Prillaman, 1982, 1988.

2. **Along the Timber Ridge Trail, 1805-1971, Lowry, VA,** Pastor William Pearson.

3. Roanoke County Public Records found in the Clerk's Office at Salem, VA.

4. Botetourt County Public Records found in the Clerk's Office at Fincastle, VA.

5. Bedford County Public Records found in the library in Bedford, VA.

6. Missouri State Historical Society Public Records found in the library, as well as **Genealogy of the Beall Families.**

7. **The Beale Papers,** James Ward, Roanoke City Library, Roanoke, VA.

8. **Gold in the Blue Ridge Mountains,** P.B. and Walter Dean Innis.

9. **The Richmond Times Dispatch,** Sunday, October 3, 1993, "Cheyenne memory fuels treasure quest," John Hoke Times-Dispatch Staff Writer
* reprinted courtesy of the Richmond Times Dispatch

10. **The Roanoke Times,** September 17, 1975, "Tavern Owners Have 'Seen' Ghost, Linda Grist Crewe.
* reprinted courtesy of the Roanoke Times

# Tavern Owners Have 'Seen' Ghost

By LINDA GRIST CREWE Times Staff Writer

MONTVALE -- At the risk of opening the proverbial can of worms, there may have been a new wrinkle added to the legendary Beale treasure mystery.

The new wrinkle comes in the form of a ghost- none other than Thomas Jefferson Beale himself who is said to have buried in 1821 the last of nearly $2 million worth of jewels, gold and silver near Buford Tavern.

Lest treasure hunters jump to conclusion, there is no proof yet that the ghost actually is T.J. Beale. But the owners of Buford Tavern have named the apparition after Beale, whose treasure has remained undiscovered for 153 years.

There is no question however, about the ghost. "He's definitely here," says Mrs. James Howell, who with her husband and son run the antique shop in Buford Tavern, once a convenient stopover for travelers to Big Lick and points west.

The Howells have lived in Buford Tavern (converted to a home many generations ago) for 11 years. They are the first family to own the house other than the Bufords.

There's no history of a ghost at Buford Tavern, but Mrs. Kitty Buford Pendleton of Roanoke says she remembers feeling "terribly uncomfortable" when she lived at Buford Tavern as a child.

"But the ghost is a new one on me," laughed Mrs. Pendleton.

"I don't remember hearinq anything about a ghost. And the feeling was iust a childhood thing."

The Howells had lived in the tavern for three or four years before they actually saw the ghost. "We knew he was here,' said Mrs. Howell. "Other than us, no one has ever seen him, but we can tell when he's here. It's just a feeling."

The feelinq that there was someone else in the house persisted until, rate one night, the Howells saw Mr. Beale.

"Like I say' my husband and I have seen him," said Mrs. Howell.

151

"It was dark, we had went to bed, but we weren't asleep yet. He came down the steps and came to the foot of our bed.

"He stood there a few m1nutes looking at us and then went on out the other door."

The Howells haven't seen Mr. Beale since that first time, but they believe he still visits the house.

"Just ask Princess," said Mrs. Howell, scratching the ears of her black toy poodle. "You know it's the funniest thing. She never barks, never growls or anything but every now and then, we'll be sitting here and she has this low growls down in her throat for the longest time. I know she senses he's in here somewhere."

Princess always faces the door on the left of the spacious room where the Howells had their bedroom on the night Mr. Beale first appeared. The door through which Beale came is located at the bottom of the stairs.

Mr. Beale doesn't live at the tavern. He wasn't there the day I visited and Mrs. Howell said she hadn't felt his presence for a couple of days.

"He always comes at night and yes, it's quite often." Said Mrs. Howell. "It's hard to tell but for a week at a time I can tell he's here and then it will go away and it'll be a while before he's back."

There are other signs of Mr. Beale. Mrs. Howell's son, Jeffrey, said things will occasionally disappear and no amount of looking can turn them up.

"Like the time my girlfriend's black leather manicure set just disappeared," he said. "She was sitting there using it and she got up to do something. When she got back Uie case was missing and we never have found it. We just don't know what happened to it."

The Howells don't question the existence of the ghost anymore, but Mrs. Howell says people think she's crazy for believing in him.

"Most of the time they look at you like you're real silly or something," she laughed. "Like you're telling them a tale."

The ghost may be real enough, but why name him Mr. Beale? It's here the story of fortune seeker Thomas Jefferson Beale comes in.

Beale, a native of Virginia, and 29 men set out on a hunting and trading expedition to Santa Fe in April 1817. Before leaving Big Lick (now Roanoke), Beale spent time at Buford Tavern.

In March 1818 the party discovered gold and in November 1819 Beale reportedly returned to Virginia to bury the gold about four miles from Buford Tavern.

The way the story goes, he returned to the west after additional gold, and made another deposit at the hidden site in December 1821. Afraid he might not return from the third trip, Beale left coded messages about the location of the treasure with Robert Morriss in Lynchburg.

In March 1822, Beale and his men left again for Santa Fe, but failed to return to Virginia. The entire party of 30 men was massacred and many scalped by Indians near the gold mining operation, according to the legend.

Only one of the three coded messages Beale left with Morriss has ever been deciphered, but treasure hunters continue to search the area around Buford Tavern and Bedford County.

"Mr. Beale has returned to look for his treasure/' said Mrs. Howell. "Now, we don't know for sure whether it 1s really Mr. Beale or not, out we have named the ghost this."

Buford Tavern would be a likely place for the ghostly Beale to reside while claiming his treasure since he is said to have spent many nights there while burying it. The tavern was used as a headquarters for the men who went west with him and Beale's bed has been preserved in the room he once used.

The tavern is located about four miles from the legendary buried treasure, making it convenient for Beale.

Then there is the matter of his dress. Mrs. Howell said he was wearing dark clothes and a wide brimmed hat when she and her husband saw him that night.

If Beale had been scalped on his last trip to Santa Fe, he might indeed wear a hat in the house even though as a gentleman he would know better. Physical descriptions of Beale say he was a tall man with dark complexion and a perfect gentleman. All this fits the feelings the Howells have about the ghost.

The ghostly feeling is strongest in Beale's old room and on the Second floor, says Mrs. Howell, but Beale is the only ghost in the house. "There is no sense that there are other ghosts," says Mrs. Howell. "There is just the one."

Others interested in the treasure have visited the tavern in search of Mr. Beale, said Mrs. Howell, but so far, no one has been successful in finding the secret to the treasure.

"We're hot afraid of him,' said Mrs. Howell. "He lives here and so do we. But, wouldn't it be nice if he told us where the treasure is," she added with a wistful laugh.

**Mrs. James Howell Straightens Ghost's Bed**

**Beale Ghost Comes Down Stairs and into the Parlor**
**Article Reprinted Courtesy of Roanoke Times - Photos by Betty Masters**

# Updated Research 2024

## Bedford Museum, Bedford, VA

Research done after the publication of "The Beale Treasure Codes, The Key," provides interesting information about the following people and places. Also, documents and photos which provide the validity of my paranormal experiences are included.

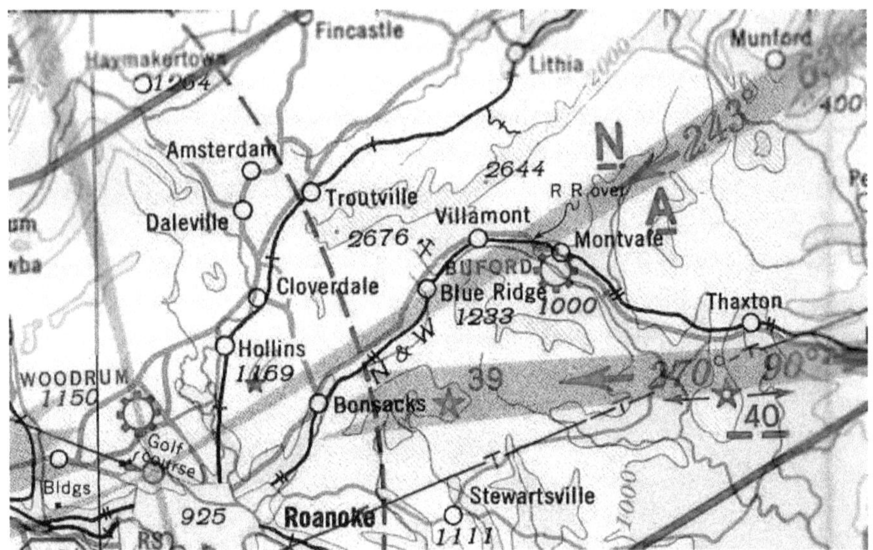



**Buford Airport, as depicted on the August 1942 Winston-Salem Sectional Chart (courtesy of Chris Kennedy). (Freeman, 2024)**

**James Buford, Montvale, Virginia in 1938 was the owner of Bufords Tavern, the Airport, and the Piper Cub airplane. This is the same airplane I talk about in Chapter 1**

1. See Chapter 2: Describes my first psychic experience where I saw a young woman standing on the back porch of "Locust Level" and the strong flow of love between us. Made me feel like she was my mother of another time. (See Henry Buford family photo, page 5, young woman 2$^{nd}$ row, to the right looks like woman standing on back porch, "Locust Level.")

2. Picture of Captain Paschal Buford (1791-1875). In this article it states Captain Paschal Buford had a daughter by the name Neeta. She was born on July 6, 1821 and died on August 26, 1826.

# Captain Paschal Buford

**1791 to 1875**

PASCHAL, son of Henry and Mildred Blackburn Buford, married Frances Ann Otey, October 31, 1820. She was the daughter of Major Isaac and Elizabeth Matthews Otey. Children - James Hervey, and Neeta (twins), born July 6, 1821, Neeta died August 26, 1826; Mildred Elizabeth, November 19, 1822; John Quincy Adams, July 29, 1824; Mary Charlotte, January 3, 1826, died July 1, 1826, died July 1, 1826; Rowland Dabney, September 20, 1827; Ann Jane, April 22, 1830; Julius Blackburn, November 22, 1832; Margaret Letitia, February 17, 1835; Isaac Henry, September 25, 1838. Paschal Buford Died at "Locust Level," Bufordville, Bedford County, Virginia, July 23, 1875, at the place of his long life.

Capt. Paschal Buford was well and widely known. His honest, outspoken nature made him a man to be remembered in social and everyday life. He had no concealments and no disguises, but spoke out with honest independence whatever was in his thoughts. For deception, pretense, or false pride he had no toleration. He was natural, and wished others to be so. He loved his broad acres, fat cattle, and blooded horses. As a farmer and breeder of fine stock, he was well known throughout the state. A lifelong success crowned his efforts in these departments of industry, and he leaves the fruits behind him in an ample estate. No Virginia home was ever the center of more generous and bounteous hospitality than his. In the War of 1812 he was an officer, and commanded a company at Crany Island. In the Civil War his hand and heart were with the South and her soldiers. By his invitation the wife (Mary) and daughter of General Robert E. Lee spent a summer (1863) at his home during the war between the states. In 1867 General Lee, then President of Washington and Lee University (Washington College at the time), accompanied by his daughter, Miss. Mildred, paid a visit to Captain Buford and his family.

Text quoted from: **History and Genealogy of the Buford Family In America** *With Records of a Number of Allied Families*

When General Lee returned to Washington College, which is located in Lexington, Virginia, Paschal Buford sent him a cow to provide milk for the family.



3. Chapter 21: My return to the childhood scene; the apparition of the little girl with long blonde hair lying in bed and appears to be dead. I believe that was Neeta Buford

4.  Use photo of Henry Buford and family. I believe the little
    girl standing in the front row with long blonde hair is Neeta
    Buford (the same little girl I saw in chapter 21).

Buford Family Photo:

**See front row, far right. The blonde girl is Neeta Buford. Behind
her standing on the right is her mother, Francis Buford.**

This is the 1870 reference for the Liberty Township of Bedford County, Virginia.

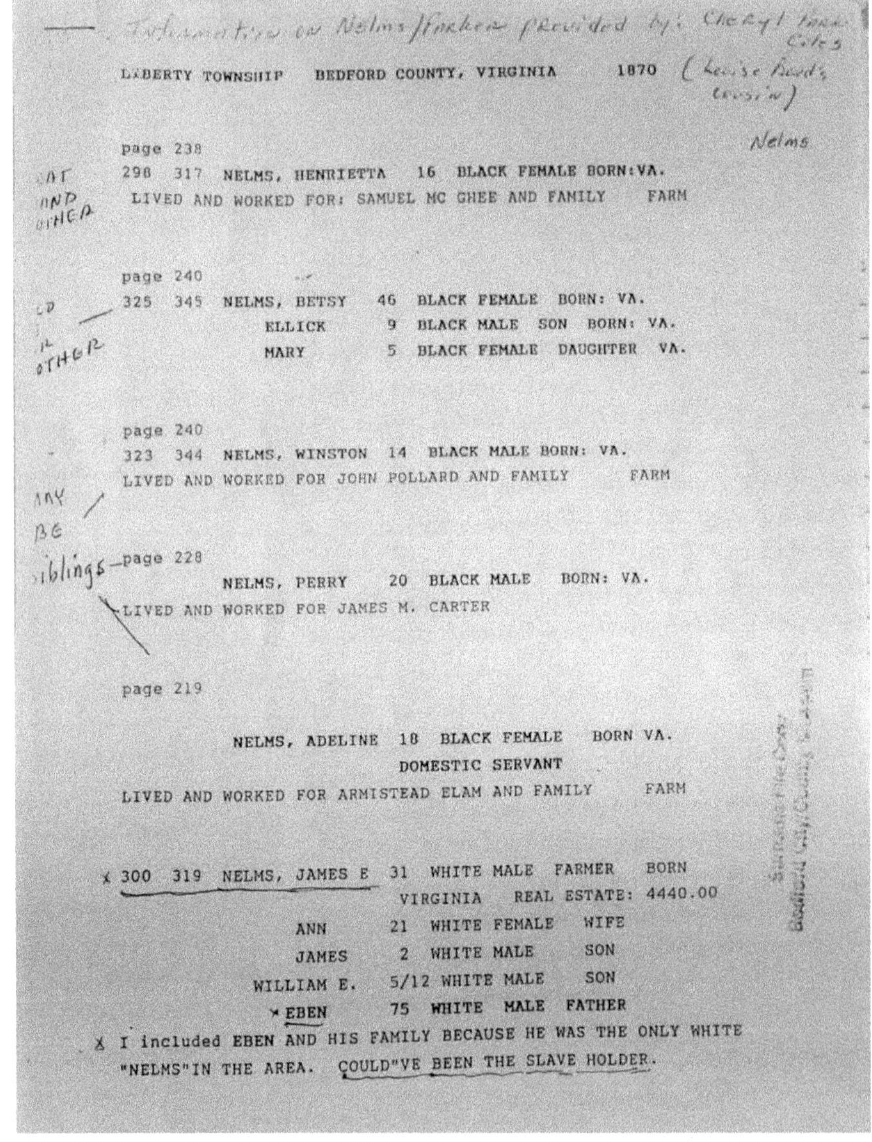

See note at bottom of page. Record for Eben Nelms and family stated they were the only "white Nelms" in the area. Said Eben could have been the slave holder.

Eben Nelms was the only man in the Beale (Beall) Treasure party who lived to be an old man and he knew where the treasure trove was.

This copy of Eben Nelms will on the following page was recorded at the Bedford Museum in Bedford, VA. The date of probation August 29, 1876 proves he lived to be an old man.

|  | | | |  |
|---|---|---|---|---|
| John Martin | 17 | 20 | Josephine L. Shaw (afs) | |
| Jeff Hancock | 10 | 20 | | |
| James B. Miller | 11 | 40 | Total cash continue from ard | $60 00 |
| Robt M. Garrett | 20 | 71 | | |
| Thomas Marion | 11 | 00 | | |
| W. P. Sherman afs | 1 | 00 | Error | 1 34 |

Josephine L. Shaw being of unsound mind, having no committee appointed, her estate bought for her a bed & bureau for which there is no [illegible]

W. P. Sherman
admr of James R. Shaw

    Sales of Tobacco in Lynchburg      12 00

    Total amount of sales      $729 55

Wm P Sherman admr
of James R. Shaw dec'd

The foregoing List Sales examined & found in proper form

J. E. Wharton Commr
of Accounts of Bedford County

At Bedford County Court Clerks Office, August 19th 1876
This List of Sales of the personal property belonging to the Estate of James R. Shaw deceased, was presented in said Office, and together with the certificate thereto annexed, admitted to record.

Teste,
[illegible] Burwell [illegible]

---

Nelms'    I Ebben Nelms of Bedford County being of sound mind
Will    and memory declare do hereby declare and make this
my writing as and for my last will & testament —

Whereas I have given to two of my sons Charles R.
Nelms & James Nelms land which I have already con-
veyed to them, which they are to hold upon the
terms specified in the deeds to them as their full share
of my lands and I intend to divide & convey the
residue of my lands to my other children in my life
time — and whereas I have given to some of my children negroes which they have lost by the [illegible]
of the late war — It is my wish & desire that in
case I should die without making any other will
that none of my children shall be held to account
in any way for any negroes that I have here-
tofore given them & that all the property that
I may own at that time other than the land
of which I am now possessed, which are to be
divided among my other children who have
had no land, shall be equally divided among
all my children then living & the descendants



163

of such as may be dead. In testimony whereof I have hereunto set my hand and seal this 20th day of May 1829

Signed sealed & acknow-          [signature]
ledged in presence of us
being both together at the
time
  [signature]
  [signature]

At Bedford Circuit Court August 24th 1829
  This last will and testament of [illegible] deceased bearing date the 20th day of May 1829, was presented in court [and] proved according to law by the oath of William [illegible] Gordon and [illegible] subscribing witnesses thereto and ordered to be recorded as the true last will and testament of said [illegible] [illegible]
                              Teste
                              [signature]

I Hannah A. Taylor of the County of Bedford State of Virginia being weak in body & of sound mind, and [illegible] memory do make and publish this as and for my last will and testament
  Item 1st It is my will that all of my just debts and funeral expenses be paid
  Item 2nd It is my will that my sister Nancy Scott shall have my household property her life, and then it is to go to my brother George W Taylor and his daughter Mary A Taylor
  Item 3rd It is my will that the remainder of my effects which is in money and bonds be deposited with George & Sipe[?] the principal of which to be kept by them and the interest of the same to be divided equally between George W Taylor and Nancy Scott [illegible] their life time. And if my brother George W Taylor should be reduced to extreme want it is my will that George & Sipe shall apply so much of the principal to him as it will take to make him comfortable and at the death of George W Taylor & Nancy Scott the [remainder] of the above mentioned bonds and money that may be left in the hand of George & Sipe[?] it is my will that my niece Mary A Taylor shall have all of it. This will signed and sealed in the presence of [illegible] and John S Preston George & Sipe[?] on the 20th day of [illegible] 18[illegible]
  Witnesses
  [signature]                   Hannah A Taylor [seal]
  John S Preston
  [signature]



164

# George Rader Brugh

In the Beale papers contained in my book, "The Beale Treasure Codes, The Key," is a letter dated May 9, 1822, sent from St. Louis, MO, by Thomas Jefferson Beale and is addressed to Robert Morris in Lynchburg, VA. In this letter Beale talks about his friend he entrusted the "key" to the treasure codes with and what to do if he failed to return in ten years to reclaim the "key."

I believe this friend was George Rader Brugh, the man I talk about in chapter five and seven in my book, "The Beale Treasure Codes, They Key."

Today, May 24, 2024, Noris Bramblett marked the grave site of George Rader Brugh for me, as shown in the photo below. Now I will move forward to try and prove his identity.

# AFFIDAVIT

I, Norris Bramblett, of Roanoke Virginia verify the following to be true.

Dowsing for old graves is the same as dowsing for water; it works for both.

I went to very old cemeteries and checked many graves and found the dowsing rods worked exceptionally well.

One grave I checked with the dowsing rods was potentially that of George Radar Brugh. The author of The Beale Treasure Codes—The Key accompanied me and showed me the location of human remains. The dowsing rods proved the location was the grave of a man.

I hereby give my consent to Claudine Fulton Ellis to use the above statement along with my photo at the grave site in her book, The Beale Treasure Codes—The Key.

_Norris Bramblett_       6/14/24
Norris Bramblett         Date

---

Commonwealth of Virginia, County of _Roanoke_

The foregoing statement was subscribed and sworn before me this _14th_ day of _June_ , 20 _24_ by _Norris Bramblett_

_Angel Rutledge Dudley_      June 14, 2024
Notary Public        Date

My commission expires on: _Nov-11/30/2026_

(SEAL)

# ABOUT THE AUTHOR

Claudine Fulton Ellis, of Scotch- Irish ancestry, was born in Bedford County, Virginia near Goose Creek Valley. She graduated high school in the Roanoke area.

Claudine says she was given a special "Gift of Sight," at birth. Although some people refer to her gift as having psychic insight, Claudine prefers to think of herself as having a special sensitivity - - especially to the spiritual world.

Claudine explains that her gift is the reason she was given knowledge about the mysteries surrounding "The Beale Papers" and the Treasure. "The revelations and research I have conducted over many decades led to writing about my experiences." She also stated, "My insight has not been limited solely to matters concerning the treasure, during my lifetime I have had numerous experiences." Except for these times, Claudine describes her life as quite normal.

Claudine was married in the mid 1950's to James Ellis. They have two children, grandchildren, and great-grandchildren.